Bilbao &
Basque
Region

Andy Symington

Credits

Footprint credits

Editor: Alan Murphy
Production and layout: Angus Dawson,
Emma Bryers
Maps: Kevin Feeney

Managing Director: Andy Riddle
Commercial Director: Patrick Dawson
Publisher: Alan Murphy
Publishing Managers: Felicity Laughton,
Nicola Gibbs.
Digital Editors: Jo Williams,
Tom Mellors
Marketing and PR: Liz Harper
Sales: Diane McEntee
Advertising: Renu Sibal
Finance and Administration:
Elizabeth Taylor

Photography credits
Front cover: Pix Achi/Shutterstock
Back cover: Toni Sanchez Poy/Shutterstock

Printed in Great Britain by CPI Antony Rowe,
Chippenham, Wiltshire

Every effort has been made to ensure that
the facts in this guidebook are accurate.
However, travellers should still obtain advice
from consulates, airlines, etc about travel
and visa requirements before travelling.
The authors and publishers cannot
accept responsibility for any loss, injury or
inconvenience however caused.

Publishing information
Footprint *Focus Bilbao & Basque Region*
1st edition
© Footprint Handbooks Ltd
August 2011

ISBN: 978 1 908206 21 3
CIP DATA: A catalogue record for this book is
available from the British Library

® Footprint Handbooks and the Footprint
mark are a registered trademark of Footprint
Handbooks Ltd

Published by Footprint
6 Riverside Court
Lower Bristol Road
Bath BA2 3DZ, UK
T +44 (0)1225 469141
F +44 (0)1225 469461
footprinttravelguides.com

Distributed in the USA by Globe Pequot
Press, Guilford, Connecticut

The content of Footprint *Focus Bilbao &
Basque Region* has been taken directly
from Footprint's *Northern Spain Handbook*
which was researched and written by Andy
Symington.

FSC
www.fsc.org

MIX
Paper from
responsible sources
FSC® C013604

Contents

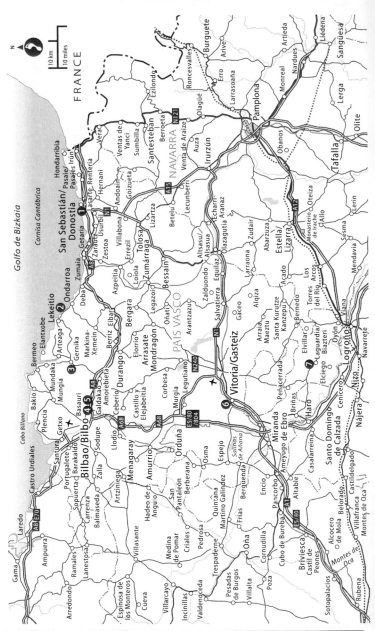

It's official: Europe's oldest people have been reborn, and everywhere the visitor looks there's some celebration or affirmation that it's good to be Basque again. Euskadi is back with a bang, and the old feeling that Bilbao is the centre of the world has rapidly returned.

Whatever your views on independence movements, Euskadi (the Basque name for this part of the world) doesn't feel very Spanish. Even the most imperialistic of the Madrid establishment refer to it as 'El País Vasco', the Basque country. The name for the region in Basque (Euskara or Euskera) is either Euskadi or Euskal Herría. Things are certainly different here; there's a strange language on road signs that would break Scrabble scoring records, weird sports are played to packed houses, it rains an awful lot and there's a subtle vibrancy that infects even the most mundane of daily tasks.

The region's biggest city, Bilbao, has managed superbly to reinvent itself from declining industrial dinosaur to optimistic European metropolis. The Guggenheim museum is a powerful symbol of this, but it's the vision and spirit that put it there that are even more invigorating. San Sebastián, meanwhile, is perennially popular for its superb natural setting and wonderful gourmet scene, and Vitoria, the peaceful Basque capital, is also very appealing.

Euskadi isn't very large, which means that most of the rural areas are within easy reach of the three cities. The rugged coast has a few excellent beaches and some very personable fishing towns. Inland, medieval towns still preserve an excellent architectural heritage, while Laguardia, by happy coincidence, is both one of the most attractive walled towns in Northern Spain and an important centre of the Rioja wine region. Outside the towns, the green hills and rocky peaks of this corner of the peninsula are an invitation into the open air.

Planning your trip

When to go

The whole of Spain is busy in July and August and, while the north isn't ridiculously crowded, you'll need to reserve rooms in advance, for which you'll be paying slightly higher prices, and significantly higher on the coast. That said, it's an enjoyable time to be in the country as there are dozens of fiestas, and everything happens outdoors. It'll be pleasantly warm on the coast and in the mountains (although you're likely to see rain in both areas), and very hot in Castilla and La Rioja – expect days in the mid to high 30s, if not higher.

June is a good time too, with milder weather and far fewer crowds, as Spanish holidays haven't started. Spring (apart from Easter week) is also quiet, and not too hot, although expect coastal showers if not serious rain. In the mountains, some routes may still be snowbound. Autumn is a good all-round time. Prices on the coast are slashed (although many hotels shut), and there are few tourists. The weather is unpredictable at this time: cool, crisp days in the mountains are likely, but on the coast you could get a week of warm sun or a fortnight of unrelenting drizzle. The cities of the interior are likely to be dry but cold – temperatures can drop below zero at night as early as October in places like Burgos and León. A bonus is that flights are cheap at these times.

In winter, temperatures are mild on the coast and cold inland. Accommodation is cheap, but many places in the mountains and on the coast are closed. Skiing starts in earnest in late January.

Getting there

Air

With budget airlines having opened up several regional airports to international flights, it's easier than ever to get to Northern Spain. **Ryanair** fly to Santiago de Compostela, Valladolid, Santander, and Zaragoza from London, while **Easyjet** serve Bilbao and Asturias, **Vueling** link Bilbao, Santiago and A Coruña with London or Edinburgh, and **Air Berlin** go to Bilbao and Asturias (among others), with a connection, from many German and Austrian airports. These airlines also run routes to other European cities. Other international airlines serve Bilbao (which is connected with London, Paris, Frankfurt, and several other European cities), Vigo, Santiago de Compostela, Zaragoza and Asturias. If you're not on the budget carriers, however, it's often cheaper to fly to Madrid and connect via a domestic flight or by land transport. Madrid is a major world airport and prices tend to be competitive.

Domestic connections via Madrid or Barcelona are frequent. **Iberia** connects Madrid with most cities of the north, while **Spanair** and **Air Europa** also operate some flights. Flights are fairly expensive, with a typical Madrid–Bilbao return costing €200. There are often specials on various websites (see below) that can bring the price down considerably. If flying into Madrid from outside Spain, an onward domestic flight can often be added at little extra cost.

While budget carriers often offer excellent value (especially when booked well ahead), they offer very little flexibility. Be aware that if you're only booking a week or so in advance, it may be cheaper with other airlines such as **British Airways** or **Iberia**. Cheap fares will usually carry a heavy financial penalty for changing dates or cancellation; check the

Don't miss...

Flying from North America and Canada To reach Northern Spain from across the Atlantic, the best way is to fly in via Madrid. From the east coast, flights can rise well over US$1400 in summer but, in winter or with advance purchase, you can get away with as little as US$600. Prices from the west coast are usually only US$100 or so more. **Iberia** flies direct to Madrid from many east coast cities and **British Airways** often offers reasonable add-on fares via London. A domestic extension from Madrid won't necessarily add much to the fare but it might be cheaper and/or more convenient getting the train. Flying in via other European hubs such as Paris or London is often less expensive, but adds a good few hours on to the journey. Travellers from Canada will sometimes find that it's cheaper to fly via London than Madrid.

Rail

Travelling from the UK to Northern Spain by train is unlikely to save either time or money; the only advantages lie in the pleasure of the journey itself, the chance to stop along the way, and the environmental impact of flying versus rail travel. Using **Eurostar** ① *T0870 160 6600, www.eurostar.com*, changing stations in Paris and boarding a TGV to Hendaye can have you in San Sebastián 10 hours after leaving Waterloo if the connections are kind. Once across the Channel, the trains are reasonably priced, but factor in £100-200 return on **Eurostar** and things don't look so rosy, unless you can take advantage of a special offer. Using the train/Channel ferry combination will more or less halve the cost and double the time.

The main rail gateway from the rest of Europe is Paris (Austerlitz). There's a Paris–Madrid sleeper daily, which stops at Vitoria, Burgos and Valladolid. Standard tourist class is €162/189 in a reclining seat/couchette to Madrid one-way, and proportionally less depending on where you get off. Check www.elipsos.com for specials. The cheaper option is to take a **TGV** from Paris to Hendaye, from where you can catch a Spanish train to San Sebastián and beyond.

For students, the **InterRail** pass is an attractive and cheap possibility, which can be obtained from travel agents, but note that the pass is not valid on the high-speed **AVE** or **EuroMed** trains. If you are planning the train journey, **Rail Europe** ① *T0844 484 064, www. raileurope.co.uk*, is a useful company. **RENFE**, Spain's rail network, has online timetables at www.renfe.es. Also see the extremely useful www.seat61.com.

Road

Bus Eurolines (www.eurolines.com) run several buses from major European cities to a variety of destinations in Northern Spain. From London, there's a bus that leaves London Victoria at 0800 on Monday and Saturday, and arrives in Bilbao at 0430 the next morning. The return leaves Bilbao at 0030 on Thursday and Saturday night, getting to London at 1945 the next evening. There's an extra bus in summer. A return fare costs about £100; it's marginally cheaper for pensioners and students, but overall isn't great value unless you're not a fan of flying. Book on T01582 404 511 or www.gobycoach.com.

Car The main route into Northern Spain is the E05/E70 motorway that runs down the southwest coast of France, crossing into Spain at Irún, near San Sebastián. More scenic but slower routes cross the Pyrenees at various points. The other motorway entrance is the E7 that runs down the east coast of Spain from France. At Barcelona you can turn inland for Lleida and Zaragoza. Both these motorways are tolled but worthwhile compared to the slow, traffic-plagued *rutas nacionales*. Most other motorways are free and in good condition.

Cars must be insured for third party and practically any driving licence is acceptable (but if you're from a country that a Guardia Civil would struggle to locate on a map, take an International Driving Licence). Unleaded petrol costs €1.10-1.25 per litre in Spain.

Sea
Bear in mind that from the UK it's usually cheaper to fly and hire a car in Northern Spain than bring the motor across on the ferry. For competitive fares by sea to France and Spain, check with **Ferrysavers** ① *T0844 576 8835, www.ferrysavers.com* and **www.ferrycheap. com**, which list special offers from various operators. The website **www.seat61.com** is good for investigating train/ferry combinations.

Now that P&O no longer run a Bilbao service, the only UK-Spain ferry is the service run by **Brittany Ferries** ① *T0871 244 0744, www.brittany-ferries.co.uk*, from Plymouth and Portsmouth to Santander. There's one weekly sailing on each route, taking around 24 hours from Portsmouth and 20 hours from Plymouth. Prices are variable but can usually be found for about £70-90 each way in a reclining seat. A car adds about £150 each way, and cabins start from about £80.

At time of writing, a trial ferry service had started up between Gijón and St Nazaire in France, potentially saving a good deal of driving. See page 402 for details.

Getting around

Public transport between the larger towns in Northern Spain is good; you can expect several buses a day between adjacent provincial capitals; these services are quick and efficient. The new network of high-speed **AVE** trains link major cities in double-quick time, but are significantly more expensive than the bus. Other train services are slow. If you want to explore much of rural Northern Spain, however, you'll probably want to hire a car, take a bike, or walk the Camino de Santiago.

Rail
The Spanish national rail network **RENFE** ① *T902 240 202 (English-speaking operators), www.renfe.es*, is, thanks to its growing network of high-speed trains, becoming a very useful option for getting around Northern Spain. **AVE** trains run from Madrid to Valladolid, Zaragoza and Huesca, with other routes under construction to nearly all of Northern Spain's major cities. These trains cover these large distances impressively quickly and reliably. It is an expensive but excellent service that refunds part or all of the ticket price if it arrives late. Elsewhere though, you'll find the bus is often quicker and cheaper than the train.

Prices vary significantly according to the type of service you are using. The standard fast-ish intercity service is called *Talgo*, while other intercity services are labelled *Altaria*, *Intercity*, *Diurno* and *Estrella* (overnight). Slower local trains are called *regionales*.

It's always worth buying a ticket in advance for long-distance travel, as trains are often full. The best option is to buy them via the website, which sometimes offers advance- purchase discounts. You can also book by phone, but they only accept Spanish cards. In either case, you get a reservation code, then print off your ticket at the terminals at the station. If buying your ticket at the station, allow plenty of time for queuing. Ticket windows are labelled *venta anticipada* (in advance) and *venta inmediata* (six hours or less before the journey). A better option can be to use a travel agent; the ones that sell tickets will display a **RENFE** sign, but you'll have to purchase them a day in advance. Commission is minimal.

All Spanish trains are non-smoking. The faster trains will have first-class (*preferente*) and second-class sections as well as a *cafetería*. First class costs about 30% more than standard and can be a worthwhile deal on a crowded long journey. Other pricing is bewilderingly complex. Night trains are more expensive, even if you don't take a sleeping berth, and there's a system of peak/off-peak days that makes little difference in practice. Buying a return ticket is 10-20% cheaper than two singles, but you qualify for this discount even if you buy the return leg later (but not on every service). A useful tip: if the train is 'full' for your particular destination, try to buy a ticket halfway (or even one stop), get on, and then ask the ticket inspector whether it's possible to go further. You may have to shuffle seats a couple of times, but most are fairly helpful – you can pay the excess fare on board. Don't board a train without a ticket though.

An **ISIC student card** or **under-26 card** grants a discount of between 20% to 30% on train services. If you're using a European railpass, be aware that you'll still have to make a reservation on Spanish trains and pay the small reservation fee (which covers your insurance).

The other important Northern Spanish network is **FEVE** ① *www.feve.es*, whose main line runs along the north coast from Bilbao to Santander, Asturias, and as far as Ferrol in Galicia; there's another line from Bilbao to León. It's a slow line, but very picturesque. It stops at many small villages and is handy for exploring the coast. They also operate the luxury *Transcantábrico*, a week's journey along the whole network, with numerous side trips, and gourmet meals. A third handy network is **Eusko Trenbideak** ① *www.euskotren.es*, a short-haul train service in the Basque country. It's an excellent service with good coverage of the inland towns.

Both **FEVE** and **RENFE** operate short-distance *cercanías* (commuter trains) in some areas, essentially suburban train services. These are particularly helpful in Asturias and around Bilbao.

Road

Bus Buses are the staple of Spanish public transport. Services between major cities are fast, frequent, reliable and fairly cheap; the five-hour trip from Madrid to Oviedo, for example, costs €31. When buying a ticket, always check how long the journey will take, as the odd bus will be an 'all stations to' job, calling in at villages that seem surprised to even see it. *Directo* is the term for a bus that doesn't stop; it won't usually cost any more either. Various premium services (called *Supra*, *Ejecutivo* or similar) add comfort, with onboard drinks service, lounge area in the bus station and more space, but cost around 60% more.

Most cities have a single terminal, the *estación de autobuses*, which is where all short- and long-haul services leave from. Buy your tickets at the relevant window; if there isn't one, buy it from the driver. Many companies don't allow baggage in the cabin of the bus, but security is pretty good. Most tickets will have a seat number (*asiento*) on them; ask when buying the ticket if you prefer a window (*ventana*) or aisle (*pasillo*) seat. There's a huge number of intercity bus companies, some of which allow phone and online booking; the most useful in Northern Spain is **ALSA** ① *T902 422 242* , *www.alsa.e*s, which is based in Asturias and runs many routes. The website www.movelia.es is also useful. The platform that the bus leaves from is called a *dársena* or *andén*. If you're travelling at busy times (particularly a fiesta or national holiday) always book the bus ticket in advance. If the bus station is out of town, there are usually travel agents in the centre who can do this for you at no extra charge.

Rural bus services are slower, less frequent and more difficult to coordinate. They typically run early in the morning and late in the evening; they're designed for villagers who visit the big city once a week or so to shop.

All bus services are reduced on Sundays and, to a lesser extent, on Saturdays; some services don't run at all on weekends. Local newspapers publish a comprehensive list of departures; expect few during siesta hours. While most large villages will have at least some bus service to their provincial capital, don't expect there to be buses running to tourist attractions like monasteries, beaches or castles; it's assumed that all tourists have cars.

Most Spanish cities have their sights closely packed into the centre, so you won't find local buses particularly necessary. There's a fairly comprehensive network in most towns, though; the Ins and outs and Transport sections in this guide indicate where they come in handy. In most cities, you just board and pay the driver.

Car The roads in Northern Spain are good, excellent in many parts. While driving isn't as sedate as in parts of Northern Europe, it's generally of a very high standard, and you'll have few problems. To drive in Spain, you'll need a full driving licence from your home country. This applies to virtually all foreign nationals, but in practice, if you're from an 'unusual' country, consider an International Driving Licence or official translation of your licence into Spanish.

There are two types of motorway in Spain, *autovías* and *autopistas*; the quality of both is generally excellent, with a speed limit of 120 kph. They are signposted in blue and may have tolls payable, in which case there'll be a red warning circle on the blue sign when you're entering the motorway. An 'A' prefix to the road number indicates a motorway; an 'AP' prefix indicates a toll motorway. Tolls are generally reasonable, but extortionate in the Basque country. You can pay by cash or card. Most motorways in Northern Spain, however, are free.

Rutas Nacionales form the backbone of Spain's road network. Centrally administered, they vary wildly in quality. Typically, they are choked with traffic backed up behind trucks, and there are few stretches of dual carriageway. Driving at siesta time is a good idea if you're going to be on a busy stretch. *Rutas Nacionales* are marked with a red 'N' number. The speed limit is 100 kph outside built-up areas, as it is for secondary roads, which are numbered with a provincial prefix (eg BU-552 in Burgos province), although some are demarcated 'B' and 'C' instead.

In urban areas, the speed limit is 50 kph. Many towns and villages have sensors that will turn traffic lights red if you're over the limit on approach. City driving can be confusing, with signposting generally poor and traffic heavy; it's worth printing off the directions that your hotel may send you with a reservation. In some towns and cities, many of the hotels are officially signposted, making things easier. Larger cities may have their historic quarter blocked off by barriers: if your hotel lies within these, ring the buzzer and say the name of the hotel, and the barriers will open.

Police are increasingly enforcing speed limits in Spain, and foreign drivers are liable to a large on-the-spot fine. Drivers can also be punished for not carrying two red warning triangles to place on the road in case of breakdown, a bulb-replacement kit and a fluorescent green waistcoat to wear if you break down by the side of the road. Drink driving is being cracked down on more than was once the case; the limit is 0.5 g/l of blood, slightly less than the equivalent in the UK, for example.

Basque sports

The best-known Basque sport is **pelota**, www.euskalpilota.com, sometimes called *jai alai*, played on a three-sided court known as a *frontón*. In the most common version, two teams of two hit the ball with their hands against the walls seeking, like squash, to prevent the other team from returning it. The ball is far from soft; after a long career players' hands resemble winning entries in a root-vegetable show. Variations of the game are *pelota a pala*, using bats, and *cesta punta*, using a wickerwork glove that can propel the ball at frightening speeds. Most courts have matches on Saturday and Sunday evenings. Confusingly, the seasons vary from town to town, but there's always something on somewhere. Other traditional Basque sports tend to be unreconstructed tests of strength, such as **wood-chopping**, or the alarming **stone-lifting**, in which stocky *harrijasotzaileak* dead-lift weights in excess of 300 kg. The best places to see these sports are at village fiestas.

Parking is a problem in nearly every town and city in Northern Spain. Red or yellow lines on the side of the street mean no parking. Blue lines indicate a metered zone, while white lines mean that some restriction is in place; a sign will give details. Parking meters can usually only be dosed up for a maximum of two hours, but they take a siesta at lunchtime too. Print the ticket off and display it in the car. Once the day's period has expired, you can charge it up for the next morning to avoid an early start. If you get a ticket, you can pay a minimal fine at the machine within the first half hour or hour instead of the full whack. Underground car parks are common and well signposted, but fairly pricey; €12-20 a day is normal. However, this is the safest option if you are going to leave any valuables in your car.

Liability insurance is required for every car driven in Spain and you must carry proof of it. If bringing your own car, check carefully with your insurers that you're covered, and get a certificate (green card). If your insurer doesn't cover you for breakdowns, consider joining the RACE ① *T902 120 441, www.race.es*, Spain's automobile association, which provides good breakdown cover.

Hiring a car in Spain is easy but not especially cheap. The major multinationals have offices at all large towns and airports; the company with the broadest network is **National/ATESA** ① *www.atesa.es*. Brokers, such as **Holiday Autos**, www.holidayautos.co.uk, are usually cheaper than booking direct with the rental companies. Prices start at around €150 per week for a small car with unlimited mileage. You'll need a credit card and most agencies will either not accept under 25s or demand a surcharge. Rates from the airports tend to be cheaper than from towns. Before booking, use a price-comparison website like www.kelkoo.com to find the best deals.

Cycling Cycling presents a curious contrast; Spaniards are mad for the competitive sport, but comparatively uninterested in cycling as a means of transport. Thus there are plenty of cycling shops but very few bike lanes, though these are rapidly being constructed in most cities in the region. By far the best places to cycle are the north coast and the Pyrenees; these are where interest in cycling is high. Trying to enjoy a Castilian highway in 40°C heat with trucks zipping past your ears is another matter, although the Camino de Santiago route is a good alternative, with long off-road sections. Contact the **Real Federación de Ciclismo en España** ① *www.rfec.com*, for more links and assistance.

Motorcycling Motorcycling is a good way to enjoy Spain and there are few difficulties to trouble the biker; bike shops and mechanics are relatively common. Hiring a motorbike, however, is difficult; there are few outlets in Northern Spain. The **Real Federación Motociclista Española** ⓘ *www.rfme.net*, can help with links and advice.

Taxis Taxis are a good option; flagfall is €2-3 in most places (it increases slightly at night and on Sundays) and it gets you a good distance. A taxi is available if its green light is lit; hail one on the street or ask for the nearest rank (*parada de taxis*). In smaller towns or at quiet times, you 'll have to ring for one. All towns have their own taxi company; phone numbers are given in the text.

Maps

The Michelin road maps are reliable for general navigation, although if you're getting off the beaten track you'll often find a local map handy. Tourist offices provide these, which vary in quality. The best topographical maps are published by the **Instituto Geográfico Nacional (IGN)**. These are not necessarily more accurate than those obtainable in Britain or North America. A useful website for route planning is www.guiarepsol.com. Car hire companies have navigation systems available, though they cost a hefty supplement.

Stanfords ⓘ *12-14 Long Acre, Covent Garden, London WC2E 9LP, T020 7836 1321, www.stanfords.co.uk*, with over 80 well-travelled staff and 40,000 titles in stock, is the world's largest map and travel bookshop. It also has a branch at 29 Corn Street, Bristol.

Sleeping

There are a reasonable number of well-equipped but characterless places on the edges or in the newer parts of towns in Spain. Similarly, chains such as NH, AC, and Hesperia have stocked Northern Spain's cities with reasonably comfortable but frequently featureless four-star business hotels. This guide has expressly minimized these in the listings, preferring to concentrate on more atmospheric options, but they are easily accessible via their websites or hotel booking brokers. If booking accommodation without this guide, always be sure to check the location if that's important to you – it's easy to find yourself a 15-minute cab ride from the town you want to be in. Having said this, the standard of accommodation in Northern Spain is very high; even the most modest of *pensiones* are usually very clean and respectable. Places to stay (*alojamientos*) are divided into three main categories; the distinctions between them follow an arcane series of regulations devised by the government.

All registered accommodations charge an 8% value-added tax (IVA); this is often included in the price at cheaper places and may be waived if you pay cash. If you have any problems, a last resort is to ask for the *libro de reclamaciones* (complaints book), an official document that, like stepping on cracks in the pavement, means uncertain but definitely horrible consequences for the hotel if anything is written in it. If you do write something in it, you have to go to the police within 24 hours and report the fact.

Hoteles, hostales and pensiones

Hoteles (marked H or HR) are graded from one to five stars and usually occupy their own building. *Hostales* (marked Hs or HsR) go from one to three stars. *Pensiones* (P) are the standard budget option, and are usually family-run flats in an apartment block. Although it's worth looking at a room before taking it, the majority are very acceptable. Spanish

Sleeping and eating price codes

Sleeping

€€€€ over €170   **€€€** €110-170   **€€** €55-110
€ under €55

These price codes refer to a standard double/twin room, inclusive of the 8% IVA (value-added tax). The rates are for high season (usually June-August).

Eating

¶¶¶ over €20   **¶¶** €10-20   **¶** under €10

Price refers to the cost of a main course for one person, without a drink.

traditions of hospitality are alive and well; even the simplest of *pensiones* will generally provide a towel and soap, and check-out time is almost uniformly a very civilized midday. Most *pensiones* will give you keys to the exterior door; if they don't, be sure to mention the fact if you plan to stay out late.

Agroturismos and casas rurales

An excellent option if you've got transport are the networks of rural homes, called a variety of things, normally *agroturismos* or *casas rurales*. Although these are under a different classification system, the standard is often as high as any country hotel. The best of them are traditional farmhouses or old village cottages. Some are available only to rent out whole, while others operate more or less as hotels. Rates tend to be excellent compared to hotels, and many offer kitchen facilities and home-cooked meals. While many are listed in the text, there are huge numbers, especially in the coastal and mountain areas. Each regional government publishes its own listings booklet, which is available at any tourist office in the area; some of the regional tourism websites also list them. The website www.toprural.com is another good place to find them. If you have a car, this can be a hugely relaxing form of holiday accommodation and a great way to meet Spaniards.

Albergues and refugios

There are a few youth hostels (*albergues*) around, but the accessible price of *pensiones* rarely makes it worth the trouble except for solo travellers. Spanish youth hostels are frequently populated by noisy schoolkids and have curfews and check-out times unsuitable for the late hours the locals keep. The exception is in mountain regions, where there are excellent *refugios*; simple hostels for walkers and climbers along the lines of a Scottish bothy, see box, page 203.

Campsites

Most campsites are set up as well-equipped holiday villages for families; many are open only in summer. While the facilities are good, they get extremely busy in peak season; the social scene is good, but sleep can be tough. They've often got playground facilities and a swimming pool; an increasing number now offer cabin or bungalow accommodation, normally a good-value option for groups or families. In other areas, camping, unless specifically prohibited, is a matter of common sense.

Eating and drinking

Nothing in Spain illustrates its differences from the rest of Europe more than its eating and drinking culture. Whether you're halfway through Sunday lunch at 1800, ordering a plate of octopus some time after midnight, snacking on *pintxos* in the street with the entire population of Bilbao doing the same around you, or watching a businessman down a hefty brandy with his morning coffee, it hits you at some point that the whole of Spanish society more or less revolves around food and drink. ▸▸ *See Food glossary, page 540.*

Eating hours are the first point of difference. Spaniards eat little for breakfast, usually just a coffee and maybe a croissant or pastry. The mid-morning coffee and piece of tortilla is a ritual, especially for office workers, and then there might be a quick bite and a drink in a bar before lunch, which is usually started between 1400 and 1530. This is the main meal of the day and the cheapest time to eat, as most restaurants offer a good-value set menu. Lunch (and dinner) is extended at weekends, particularly on Sundays, when the *sobremesa* (chatting over the remains of the meal) can go on for hours. Most folk head home for the meal during the working week and get back to work about 1700; some people have a nap (the famous siesta), some don't. It's common to have an evening drink or *tapa* in a bar after the *paseo*, if this is extended into a food crawl it's called a *txikiteo* (Basque country) or *tapeo*. Dinner (*cena*) is normally eaten from about 2200 onwards, although sitting down to dinner at midnight at weekends isn't unusual. In smaller towns, however, and midweek you might not get fed after 2200. Be aware that any restaurant open for dinner before 2030 could well be a tourist trap. After eating, *la marcha* (the nightlife) hits drinking bars (*bares de copas*) and then nightclubs (*discotecas*; a *club* is a brothel). Many of these places only open at weekends and are usually busiest from 0200 onwards.

Eating and drinking hours vary between regions. Week nights are quieter but particularly so in the Basque country and in rural areas, where many restaurants close their kitchens at 2200. Bar food changes across the area too. In the Basque country, *pintxos* (bar-top snacks) are the way forward; in León or Salamanca a free small plate of food accompanies the smallest drink; while in some other places you'll have to order *raciones* (full plates of tapas).

Food

While the regional differences in the cuisine of Northern Spain are important, the basics remain the same. Spanish cooking relies on meat, fish/seafood, beans and potatoes given character by the chef's holy trinity: garlic, peppers and, of course, olive oil. The influence of the colonization of the Americas is evident, and the result is a hearty, filling style of meal ideally washed down with some of the nation's excellent red wines.

Regional specialities are described in the main text, but the following is an overview of the most common dishes.

Even in areas far from the coast, the availability of good **fish and seafood** can be taken for granted. *Merluza* (hake) is the staple fish, but is pushed hard by *bacalao* (salt cod) on the north coast. A variety of farmed white fish are also increasingly popular. *Gambas* (prawns) are another common and excellent choice, backed up by a bewildering array of molluscs and crustaceans as well as numerous tasty fish. Calamari, squid and cuttlefish are common; if you can cope with the slightly slimy texture, *pulpo* (octopus) is particularly good, especially when simply boiled *a la gallega* (Galician style) and flavoured with paprika and olive oil. Supreme among the seafood are *rodaballo* (turbot) and *rape* (monkfish/anglerfish). Fresh trout from the mountain streams of Navarra or Asturias are hard to beat too; they are commonly cooked with bacon or ham (*trucha a la navarra*).

Wherever you go, you'll find cured ham (*jamón serrano*), which is always excellent, but particularly so if it's the pricey *ibérico*, taken from acorn-eating porkers in Salamanca, Extremadura and Huelva. Other cold **meats** to look out for are *cecina*, made from beef and, of course, *embutidos* (sausages), including the versatile *chorizo*. Pork is also popular as a cooked meat; its most common form is sliced loin (*lomo*). The Castilian plains specialize in roast suckling pig (*cochinillo* or *lechón*), usually a sizeable dish indeed. *Lechazo* is the lamb equivalent, popular around Aranda de Duero in particular. Beef is common throughout; cheaper cuts predominate, but the better steaks (*solomillo, entrecot, chuletón*) are usually superbly tender. Spaniards tend to eat them rare (*poco hecho*; ask for *al punto* for medium-rare or *bien hecho* for well done). The *chuletón* is worth a mention in its own right; a massive T-bone best taken from an ox (*de buey*) and sold by weight, which often approaches a kilogram. It's an imposing slab of meat, best shared between two or three unless you're especially peckish. *Pollo* (chicken) is common, but usually unremarkable (unless its free-range – *pollo de corral* – in which case it's superb); game birds such as *codorniz* (quail) and *perdiz* (partridge) as well as *pato* (duck) are also widely eaten. The innards of animals are popular; *callos* (tripe), *mollejas* (sweetbreads) and *morcilla* (black pudding in solid or liquid form) are all excellent, if acquired, tastes. Fans of the unusual will be keen to try *jabalí* (wild boar), *potro* (foal), *morros* (pig cheeks) and *oreja* (ear, usually from a pig or sheep).

Main dishes often come without any **accompaniments**, or chips at best. The consolation, however, is the *ensalada mixta*, whose simple name (mixed salad) often conceals a meal in itself. The ingredients vary, but it's typically a plentiful combination of lettuce, tomato, onion, olive oil, boiled eggs, asparagus, olives and tuna. The *tortilla* (a substantial potato omelette) is ever-present and often excellent. *Revueltos* (scrambled eggs), are usually tastily combined with prawns, asparagus or other goodies. Most **vegetable** dishes are based around that New World trio: the bean, the pepper and the potato. There are numerous varieties of bean in Northern Spain; they are normally served as some sort of hearty stew, often with bits of meat or seafood. *Fabada* is the Asturian classic of this variety, while *alubias con chorizo* are a standard across the region. A *cocido* is a typical mountain dish, a massive stew of chickpeas or beans with meat and vegetables; the liquid is drained off and eaten first (*sopa de cocido*). Peppers (*pimientos*), too, come in a number of forms. As well as being used to flavour dishes, they are often eaten in their own right; *pimientos rellenos* come stuffed with meat or seafood. Potatoes come as chips, *bravas* (with a garlic or spicy tomato sauce) or *a la riojana*, with chorizo and paprika. Other common vegetable dishes include *menestra* (delicious blend of cooked vegetables), which usually has some ham in it, and *ensaladilla rusa*, a tasty blend of potato, peas, peppers, carrots and mayonnaise. *Setas* (wild mushrooms) are a delight, particularly in autumn.

Desserts focus on the sweet and milky. *Flan* (a sort of crème caramel) is ubiquitous; great when *casero* (home-made), but often out of a plastic tub. *Natillas* are a similar but more liquid version, and *arroz con leche* is a cold, sweet, rice pudding typical of Northern Spain. **Cheeses** tend to be bland or salty and are normally eaten as a tapa or entrée. There are some excellent cheeses in Northern Spain, however; piquant Cabrales and Basque Idiázabal stand out.

Regional cuisine

Regional styles tend to use the same basic ingredients treated in slightly different ways, backed up by some local specialities. Most of Spain grudgingly concedes that Basque cuisine is the peninsula's best, the San Sebastián twilight shimmers with Michelin stars, and chummy all-male *txokos* gather in private to swap recipes and cook up feasts in members-only kitchens. But what strikes the visitor first are the *pintxos*, a stunning range of bartop snacks that in many cases seem too pretty to put your teeth in. The base of most Basque dishes is seafood, particularly *bacalao* (salt cod; occasionally stunning but often ordinary), and the region has taken full advantage of its French ties.

Navarran and Aragonese cuisine owes much to the mountains, with hearty stews and game dishes featuring alongside fresh trout. Rioja and Castilla y León go for filling roast meat and bean dishes more suited to the harsh winters than the baking summers. Asturias and Cantabria are seafood-minded on the coast but search for more warming fare in the high ground, and Galicia is seafood heaven, with more varieties of finny and shelly things than you knew existed; usually prepared with confidence in the natural flavours; the rest of the area tends to overuse the garlic. Inland Galicia relies more heavily on that traditional northern staple, pork.

Food-producing regions take their responsibilities seriously, and competition is fierce. Those widely acknowledged to produce the best will often add the name of the region to the foodstuff (many foods, like wines, have denomination of origin status, DO, given by a regulatory body). Thus *pimientos de Padrón* (Padrón peppers), *cogollos de Tudela* (lettuce hearts from Tudela), *alubias de Tolosa* (Tolosa beans), *puerros de Sahagún* (Sahagún leeks) and a host of others.

Eating out

One of the great pleasures of travelling in Northern Spain is eating out, but it's no fun sitting in an empty restaurant so adapt to the local hours as much as you can; it may feel strange leaving dinner until 2200, but you'll miss out on a lot of atmosphere if you don't.

The standard distinctions of bar, café and restaurant don't apply in Spain. Many places combine all three functions, and it's not always evident; the dining room (*comedor*) is often tucked away behind the bar or upstairs. *Restaurantes* are restaurants, and will usually have a dedicated dining area with set menus and à la carte options. Bars and cafés will often display food on the counter, or have a list of tapas; bars tend to be known for particular dishes they do well. Many bars, cafés and restaurants don't open on Sunday nights, and most are closed one other night a week, most commonly Monday or Tuesday.

Cafés will usually provide some kind of **breakfast** fare in the mornings; croissants and sweet pastries are the norm; freshly squeezed orange juice is also common. About 1100 they start putting out savoury fare; maybe a *tortilla*, some *ensaladilla rusa* or little ham rolls in preparation for pre-lunch snacking. It's a workers' tradition – from labourers to executives – to drop down to the local bar around 1130 for a *pincho de tortilla* (slice of potato omelette) to get them through until two.

Lunch is the biggest meal of the day for most people in Spain, and it's also the cheapest time to eat. Just about all restaurants offer a *menú del día*, which is usually a set three-course meal that includes wine or soft drink. In unglamorous workers' locals this is often as little as €8; paying anything more than €13 indicates the restaurant takes itself quite seriously. There's often a choice of several starters and mains. To make the most of the meal, a tip is to order another starter in place of a main; most places are quite happy to do it, and the starters are usually more interesting than the mains, which in the cheaper places tend to be slabs of mediocre meat. Most places open for lunch at about 1300, and stop serving at 1500 or 1530, although at weekends this can extend; it's not uncommon to see people still lunching at 1800 on a Sunday. The quality of à la carte is usually higher than the *menú*, and quantities are larger. Simpler restaurants won't offer this option except in the evenings. **Tapas** has changed in meaning over the years, and now basically refers to all bar food. This range includes free snacks given with drinks (now only standard in León and a few other places), *pinchos/pintxos*, see box, page 106, small saucer-sized plates of food (this is the true meaning of *tapa*) and more substantial dishes, usually ordered in *raciones* and designed to be shared. A *ración* in Northern Spain is no mean affair; it can often comfortably fill one person, so if you want to sample a range of things, you're better to ask for a half (*media*) or a *tapa* (smaller portion, when available). Prices of *raciones* basically depend on the ingredients; a good portion of *langostinos* (king prawns) will likely set you back €12, while more *morcilla* (black pudding) or *patatas* than you can eat might only be €4 or so.

Most restaurants open for dinner at 2030 or later. Although some places do offer a cheap set *menú*, you'll usually have to order à la carte. In quiet areas, places stop serving at 2200 on week nights, but in cities and at weekends people sit down at 2230 or later. A cheap option at all times is a *plato combinado*, most commonly offered in cafés. They're usually a greasy spoon-style mix of eggs, steak, bacon and chips or similar and are filling but rarely inspiring.

Vegetarians in Spain won't be spoiled for choice, but at least what there is tends to be good. There's a small but rapidly increasing number of dedicated vegetarian restaurants, but most other places won't have a vegetarian main course on offer, although the existence of *raciones* and salads makes this less of a burden than it might be. *Ensalada mixta* nearly always has tuna in it, but it's usually made fresh, so places will happily leave it out. *Ensaladilla rusa* is normally a good bet, but ask about the tuna too, just in case. Tortilla is simple but delicious and ubiquitous. Simple potato or pepper dishes are tasty options (although beware of peppers stuffed with meat), and many *revueltos* (scrambled eggs) are just mixed with asparagus. Annoyingly, most vegetable *menestras* are seeded with ham before cooking, and bean dishes usually contain at least some meat or animal fat. You'll have to specify *soy vegetariano/a* (I am a vegetarian), but ask what dishes contain, as ham, fish and chicken are often considered suitable vegetarian fare. Vegans will have a tougher time. What doesn't have meat nearly always contains cheese or egg. Better restaurants, particularly in cities, will be happy to prepare something to guidelines, but otherwise better stick to very simple dishes.

Drink

In good Catholic fashion, **wine** is the lifeblood of Spain. It's the standard accompaniment to most meals, but also features very prominently in bars, where a glass of cheap *tinto* or *blanco* can cost as little as €0.80, although it's more normally €1.20. A bottle of house wine in a restaurant is often no more than €5 or €6. *Tinto* is red (although if you just order *vino* it's assumed that's what you want); *blanco* is white, and rosé is either *clarete* or *rosado*. A well-regulated system of *denominaciones de origen* (DO), similar to the French *appelation controlée* has lifted the reputation of Spanish wines high above the party plonk status they once enjoyed. Much of Spain's wine is produced in the north, and recent years have seen regions such as the Ribera del Duero, Rueda, Navarra, Toro, Bierzo, and Rías Baixas achieve worldwide recognition. But the daddy, of course, is still Rioja.

The overall standard of Riojas has improved markedly since the granting of the higher DOC status in 1991, with some fairly stringent testing in place. Red predominates; these are mostly medium-bodied bottles from the Tempranillo grape (with three other permitted red grapes often used to add depth or character). Whites from Viura and Malvasia are also produced: the majority of these are young, fresh and dry, unlike the traditional powerful oaky Rioja whites now on the decline. Rosés are also produced. The quality of individual Riojas varies widely according to both producer and the amount of time the wines have been aged in oak barrels and in the bottle. The words *crianza*, *reserva* and *gran reserva* refer to the length of the ageing process (see box, above), while the vintage date is also given. Rioja producers store their wines at the bodega until deemed ready for drinking, so it's common to see wines dating back a decade or more on shelves and wine lists.

A growing number of people feel, however, that Spain's best reds come from further west, in the Ribera del Duero region east of Valladolid. The king's favourite tipple, Vega Sicilia, has long been Spain's most prestigious wine, but other producers from the area have also gained stellar reviews.

Visiting the area in the baking summer heat, it's hard to believe that nearby Rueda can produce quality whites, but it certainly does. Most come from the Verdejo grape and have an attractive, dry, lemony taste; Sauvignon Blanc has also been planted with some success.

Galicia produces some excellent whites too; the coastal Albariño vineyards produce a sought-after dry wine with a very distinctive bouquet. Ribeiro is another good Galician white, and the reds from there are also tasty, having some similarity to those produced in nearby northern Portugal. Ribeira Sacra is another inland Galician denomination producing whites and reds from a wide range of varietals.

Among other regions, Navarra, long known only for rosé, is producing some quality red wines unfettered by the stricter rules governing production in Rioja, while Bierzo, in western León province, also produces interesting wines from the red Prieto Picudo and Mencía grapes. Other DO wines in Northern Spain include Somontano, a red and white appellation from Aragón and Toro, whose baking climate makes for full-bodied reds. Some Toro wines have achieved a very high worldwide profile.

An unusual wine worth trying is *txakolí*, with a small production on the Basque coast. The most common is a young, refreshing, acidic white which has a green tinge and slight sparkle, often accentuated by pouring from a height. The best examples, from around Getaria, go well with seafood. The wine is made from under-ripe grapes of the Ondarrubi Zuria variety; there's a less common red species and some rosé.

One of the joys of Spain, though, is the rest of the wine. Order a *menú del día* at a cheap restaurant and you'll be unceremoniously served a cheap bottle of local red (sometimes without even asking for it). Wine snobbery can leave by the back door at this point: it may be cold, but you'll find it refreshing; it may be acidic, but once the olive-oil laden food arrives, you'll be glad of it. It's not there to be judged, it's a staple like bread and, like bread, it's sometimes excellent, it's sometimes bad, but mostly it fulfils its purpose perfectly. Wine is not a luxury item in Spain, so people add water to it if they feel like it, or lemonade (*gaseosa*), or *cola* (to make the party drink called *calimocho*). Tinto de verano is a summer slurper similar to sangría, a mixture of red wine, gaseosa, ice, and optional fruit.

In most bars, you can order Rioja, Ribera, Rueda, or other regions by the glass (usually €1.20-2.50). If you ask for *crianza* or *reserva*, you'll usually get a Rioja. A *tinto* or *blanco* will usually get you a cheapish local wine, sometimes excellent, sometimes awful. As a general rule, only bars serving food serve wine; most *pubs* and *discotecas* won't have it.

Spanish **beer** is mostly lager, usually reasonably strong, fairly gassy, cold and good. On the tapas trail, many people order *cortos* (*zuritos* in the Basque lands), usually about 100 ml. A *caña* is a larger draught beer, usually about 200 ml. Order a *cerveza* and you'll get a bottled beer. Many people order their beer *con gas*, topped up with mineral water, sometimes called a *clara*, although this normally means it's topped with lemonade. In some pubs, particularly those specializing in different beers (*cervecerías*), you can order pints (*pintas*).

Cider (*sidra*) is an institution in Asturias, and to a lesser extent in Euskadi. The cider is flat, sour and yeasty; the appley taste will be a surprise after most commercial versions of the drink. Asturias' *sidrerías* offer some of Spain's most enjoyable bar life, see box, page 415, with excellent food, a distinctive odour, sawdust on the floor, and the cider poured from above head height by uniformed waiters to give it some bounce. In Euskadi in springtime, people decamp to cider houses in the hills to eat massive meals and serve themselves bottomless glasses of the stuff direct from the vat.

Spirits are cheap in Spain. Vermouth (*vermut*) is a popular pre-lunch *aperitif*, as is *patxarán* (see glossary, page 540). Many bars make their own vermouth by adding various herbs and fruits and letting it sit in barrels; this can be excellent, particularly if its from a *solera*. This is a system where liquid is drawn from the oldest of a series of barrels, which is then topped up with the next oldest, resulting in a very mellow characterful drink. After dinner or lunch it's time for a *copa*: people relax over a whisky or a brandy, or hit the mixed drinks (*cubatas*): *gin tonic* is obvious, as is *vodka con cola*. Spirits are free-poured and large; don't be surprised at a 100 ml measure. A mixed drink costs €3.50-6. Whisky is popular, and most bars have a good range. Spanish brandy is good, although its oaky vanilla flavours don't appeal to everyone. There are numerous varieties of rum and flavoured liqueurs. When ordering a spirit, you'll be expected to choose which brand you want; the local varieties (eg *Larios* gin, *DYC* whisky) are marginally cheaper than their imported brethren but lower in quality. *Chupitos* are shots; restaurants will often throw in a free one at the end of a meal, or give you a bottle of *orujo* (grape spirit) to pep up your black coffee.

Juice is normally bottled and expensive; *mosto* (grape juice; really pre-fermented wine) is a cheaper and popular soft drink in bars. There's the usual range of **fizzy drinks** (*gaseosas*) available. *Horchata* is a summer drink, a sort of milkshake made from tiger nuts. **Water** (*agua*) comes *con* (with) or *sin* (without) *gas*. The tap water is totally safe to drink, but it's not always the nicest; many Spaniards drink bottled water at home.

Coffee (*café*) is usually excellent and strong. *Solo* is black, mostly served espresso style. Order *americano* if you want a long black, *cortado* if you want a dash of milk, or *con leche* for about half milk. A *carajillo* is a coffee with brandy, while *queimado* – a Galician drink of ritual significance – is a mixture of coffee and *orujo* (grape spirit), made in a huge vessel. **Tea** (*té*) is served without milk unless you ask; herbal teas (*infusiones*) are common, especially chamomile (*manzanilla*) and mint (*menta poleo*). **Chocolate** is a reasonably popular drink at breakfast time or in the afternoon (*merienda*), served with *churros*, fried doughsticks that seduce about a quarter of visitors and repel the rest.

Festivals and events

Fiestas
Even the smallest village in Spain has a fiesta, and some have several. Although mostly nominally religious in nature, they usually include the works; a mass and procession or two to be sure, but also live music, bullfights, competitions, fireworks and copious drinking of *calimocho/kalimotxo*, a mix of red wine and cola (not as bad as it sounds). A feature of many are the *gigantes y cabezudos*, huge-headed papier-mâché figures based on historical personages who parade the streets. Adding to the sense of fun are *penas*, boisterous social clubs who patrol the streets making music, get rowdy at the bullfights and drink wine all night and day. Most fiestas are in summer, and if you're spending much time in Spain in that period you're bound to run into one; expect some trouble finding accommodation. Details of the major town fiestas can be found in the travel text. National holidays and long weekends (*puentes*) can be difficult times to travel; it's important to reserve tickets in advance.

Essentials A-Z

Accident and emergency
There are various emergency numbers, but the general one across the nation is now T112. This will get you the police, ambulance, or fire brigade. T091 gets just the police.

Children
Kids are kings in Spain, and it's one of the easiest places to take them along on holiday. Children socialize with their parents from an early age here, and you'll see them eating in restaurants and out in bars well after midnight. The outdoor summer life and high pedestrianization of the cities is especially suitable and stress-free for both you and the kids to enjoy the experience.

Spaniards are friendly and accommodating towards children, and you'll undoubtedly get treated better with them than without, except perhaps in the most expensive restaurants and hotels. Few places, however, are equipped with highchairs, unbreakable plates or baby-changing facilities. Children are expected to eat the same food as their parents, although you'll sometimes see a *menú infantil* at a restaurant, which typically has simpler dishes and smaller portions.

The cut-off age for children paying half or no admission/passage on public transport and in tourist attractions varies widely. **RENFE** trains let children under 4 travel for free, and its discount passage of around 50% applies up to the age of 12. Most car rental companies have child seats available, but it's wise to book these in advance.

As for attractions, beaches are an obvious highlight, but many of the newer museums are hands-on, and playgrounds and parks are common. Campsites cater to families and the larger ones often have child-minding facilities and activities.

Customs and duty-free
Non-EU citizens are allowed to import 1 litre of spirits, 2 litres of wine and 200 cigarettes or 250 g of tobacco or 50 cigars. EU citizens are theoretically limited by personal use only though individual countries may specify what they regard this as being.

Electricity
Spain uses the standard European 220V plug, with 2 round pins.

Health
Health for travellers in Spain is rarely a problem. Medical facilities are good, and the worst most travellers experience is an upset stomach, usually merely a result of the different diet rather than any bug.

The water is safe to drink, but isn't always that pleasant, so many travellers (and locals) stick to bottled water. The sun in Spain can be harsh, so take adequate precautions to prevent heat exhaustion/sunburn. Many medications that require a prescription in other countries are available over the counter at pharmacies in Spain. Pharmacists are highly trained but don't necessarily speak English. In all medium-sized towns and cities, at least one pharmacy is open 24 hrs; this is organized on a rota system; details are posted in the window of all pharmacies and in local newspapers.

Insurance
British and other European citizens should get hold of a **European Health Insurance Card** (**EHIC**), available via www.dh.gov. uk or from post offices in the UK, before leaving home. This guarantees free medical care throughout the EU. Other citizens should seriously consider medical insurance, but check for reciprocal Spanish cover with your private or public health scheme first.

Insurance is a good idea anyway to cover you for theft, etc. In the event of theft, you'll have to make a report at the local police station within 24 hrs and obtain a report to show your insurers. (English levels at the police station are likely to be low, so try to take a Spanish speaker with you to help).

Language

For travelling purposes, everyone in Northern Spain speaks Spanish, known either as *castellano* or *español*, and it's a huge help to know some. Most young people know some English, and standards are rapidly rising, but don't assume that people aged 40 or over know any at all. Spaniards are often shy to attempt to speak English. While many visitor attractions have some sort of information available in English (and to a lesser extent French and German), many don't, or have English tours only in times of high demand. Most tourist office staff will speak at least some English, and there's a good range of translated information available in most places. See page 536 for useful words and phrases in Spanish.

While efforts to speak the language are appreciated, it's more or less expected, to the same degree as English is expected in Britain or the USA. Nobody will be rude if you don't speak any Spanish, but nobody will think to slow their rapidfire stream of the language for your benefit either, or pat you on the back for producing a few phrases in their tongue.

The other languages you'll come across in Northern Spain are *Euskara/Euskera* (the Basque language), *Galego* (Galician), *Bable* (the Asturian dialect) and perhaps *Aragonés*. (Aragonese). Euskara is wholly unrelated to Spanish; if you're interested in Basque culture, by all means learn a few words (and make instant friends), but be aware that many people in Euskadi aren't Basque, and that it's quite a political issue. Bable and Galego are more similar to Spanish, but you won't need to learn any to travel in the regions.

Money → *€1 = £0.89/US$1.46 (Jun 2011).*
Currency
In 2002, Spain switched to the euro, bidding farewell to the peseta. The euro (E) is divided into 100 *céntimos*. Euro notes are standard across the whole zone, and come in denominations of 5, 10, 20, 50, 100, and the rarely seen 200 and 500. Coins have one standard face and one national face; all coins are, however, acceptable in all countries. The coins are slightly difficult to tell apart when you're not used to them. The coppers are 1, 2 and 5 cent pieces, the golds are 10, 20 and 50, and the silver/gold combinations are €1 and €2. The exchange rate at the switchover was approximately €6 to 1000 pesetas or 166 pesetas to the euro. So if someone says they paid *cien mil*, they probably mean 100,000 pesetas; €600. People still tend to think in pesetas when talking about large amounts like house prices.

ATMs and banks
The best way to get money in Spain is by plastic. ATMs are plentiful in Spain, and just about all of them accept all the major international debit and credit cards. The Spanish bank won't charge for the transaction, though they will charge a mark-up on the exchange rate, but beware of your own bank hitting you for a hefty fee: check with them before leaving home. Even if they do, it's likely to be a better deal than exchanging cash. The website www.moneysavingexpert.com has a good rundown on the most economical ways of accessing cash while travelling.

Banks are usually open 0830-1400 Mon-Fri (and Sat in winter) and many change foreign money (sometimes only the central branch in a town will do it). Commission rates vary widely; it's usually best to change large amounts, as there's often a minimum commission of €6 or so. Nevertheless, banks nearly always give better rates than change offices (*casas de cambio*), which are fewer by the day. If you're stuck outside banking hours, some large department stores such as the Corte Inglés change money at knavish rates. Traveller's cheques are accepted in many shops, although they are far less common than they were.

Tax

Nearly all goods and services in Spain are subject to a value-added tax (IVA). This is only 8% for most things the traveller will encounter, including food and hotels, but is as high as 18% on some things. IVA is normally included in the stated prices. You're technically entitled to claim it back if you're a non-EU citizen, for purchases over €90. If you're buying something pricey, make sure you get a stamped receipt clearly showing the IVA component, as well as your name and passport number; you can claim the amount back at major airports on departure. Some shops will have a form to smooth the process.

Cost of living and travelling

Prices have soared since the euro was introduced; some basics rose by 50-80% in 3 years, and hotel and restaurant prices can even seem dear by Western European standards these days. Spain's average monthly salary of €1300 is low by EU standards, and the minimum monthly salary of €600 is very low indeed.

Spain can still be a reasonably cheap place to travel if you're prepared to forgo a few luxuries. If you're travelling as a pair, staying in cheap *pensiones*, eating a set meal at lunchtime, travelling short distances by bus or train daily, and snacking on tapas in the evenings, €65 per person per day is reasonable. If you camp and grab picnic lunches from shops, you could reduce this considerably. In a cheap hotel or good *hostal* and using a car, €130 each a day and you'll not be counting pennies; €250 per day and you'll be very comfy indeed unless you're staying in 4- or 5-star accommodation.

Accommodation is more expensive in summer than in winter, particularly on the coast. The Basque lands are significantly more expensive year-round than the rest of Northern Spain, particularly for sleeping, eating and drinking. The news isn't great for the solo traveller: single rooms tend not to be particularly good value, and they are in short supply. Prices range from 60% to 80% of the double/twin price; some establishments even charge the full rate. If you're going to be staying in 3- to 5-star hotels, booking them ahead on internet discount sites can save a lot of money.

Public transport is generally cheap; intercity bus services are quick and low-priced and trains are reasonable, though the fast AVE trains cost substantially more.

Petrol is relatively cheap: standard unleaded petrol is around €1.20 per litre and diesel around €1.10. In some places, particularly in tourist areas, you may be charged up to 20% more to sit outside a restaurant. It's also worth checking if the 8% IVA (sales tax) is included in menu prices, especially in the more expensive restaurants; it should say on the menu whether this is the case.

Post

The Spanish post is notoriously inefficient and slow by European standards. Post offices (*correos*) generally open Mon-Fri 0800-1300, 1700-2000; Sat 0800-1300, although main offices in large towns stay open all day. Stamps can be bought here or at tobacconists (*estancos*). A letter or postcard within Spain costs €0.39, within Europe €1.07, and elsewhere €1.38.

Safety

Northern Spain is generally a very safe place. While port cities like Bilbao, Vigo and Santander have some dodgy areas, tourist crime is very low in this region, and you're more likely to have something returned (that you left on that train) than something stolen. That said, don't invite crime by leaving luggage or cash in cars. If parking in a city or, particularly, a popular hiking zone, try to make it clear there's nothing to nick inside by opening the glovebox, etc. Muggings are very rare, but don't leave bags unattended.

There are several types of police, helpful enough in normal circumstances. The paramilitary **Guardia Civil** dress in green and are responsible for the roads (including speed traps and the like), borders and law enforcement away from towns. They're not a bunch to get the wrong side of but are polite to tourists and have thankfully lost the bizarre winged hats they used to sport. The **Policía Nacional** are responsible for most urban crimefighting. Brown-shirted folk, these are the ones to go to if you need to report anything stolen, etc. **Policía Local/Municipal** are present in large towns and cities and are responsible for some urban crime, as well as traffic control and parking. The **Ertzaintza** are the most dashing force in Spain, with cocky red berets. They are a Basque force who deal with the day-to-day beat and some crime. There's a similar corps in Navarra.

Telephone → *Country code +34.*
There's a public telephone in many bars, but hearing the conversation over the ambient noise can be a hard task and rates are slightly higher than on the street. Phone booths on the street are mostly operated by **Telefónica**, and all have international direct dialling (00 is the prefix for international calls). They accept coins from €0.05 upwards and phone cards, which can be bought from *estancos*.

For directory enquiries, dial T11818 for national or T11825 for international numbers. The local operator is on T1009 and the international one on T1008.

Domestic landlines have 9-digit numbers beginning with 9 (occasionally with 8). Although the first 3 digits indicate the province, you have to dial the full number from wherever you are calling, including abroad. Mobiles numbers start with 6.

Mobiles (*móviles*) are big in Spain and coverage is very good. Most foreign mobiles will work in Spain (although older North American ones won't); check with your service provider about what the call costs will be like. Many mobile networks require you to call up before leaving your home country to activate overseas service ('roaming'). If you're staying a while, it may be cheaper to buy a Spanish mobile or SIM card, as there are always numerous offers and discounts.

Time
Spain operates on western European time, ie GMT +1, and changes its clocks in line with the rest of the EU.

'Spanish time' isn't as elastic as it used to be, but if you're told something will happen *'enseguida'* ('straight away') it may take 10 mins, if you're told *'cinco minutos'* (5 mins), grab a seat and a book. Transport, especially buses, leaves promptly.

Tipping
Tipping in Spain is far from compulsory, but much practised. Around 10% is considered extremely generous in a restaurant; 3-5% is more usual. It's rare for a service charge to be added to a bill. Waiters do not normally expect tips for lunchtime set meals or tapas, but here and in bars and cafés people will often leave small change, especially for table service. Taxi drivers don't expect a tip, but will be pleased to receive one. In rural areas, churches will often have a local keyholder who will open it up for you; if there's no admission charge, a tip or donation is appropriate (say €1 per head; more if they've given a detailed tour).

Tourist information
The tourist information infrastructure in Northern Spain is organized by the regional governments and is generally excellent, with a wide range of information, often in English, German and French as well as Spanish. Offices within the region can provide maps of the area and towns, and lists of registered accommodation, usually

with 1 booklet for hotels, *hostales*, and *pensiones*; another for campsites, and another, especially worth picking up, listing farmstay and rural accommodation, which has taken off in a big way; hundreds are added yearly. Opening hours are longer in major cities; many rural offices are only open in summer. Average opening hours are Mon-Sat 1000-1400, 1600-1900, Sun 1000-1400. Offices are often closed on Sun or Mon. Staff often speak English and other European languages and are well trained. The offices (*oficinas de turismo*) are often signposted to some degree within the town or city. Staff may ask where you are from; this is not nosiness but for statistical purposes.

País Vasco (Euskadi),
www.turismoa.euskadi.net

Other useful websites

www.alsa.es Northern Spain's major bus operator. Book online.

www.bilbao.net The city's excellent website.

www.cyberspain.com Good background on culture and fiestas.

www.elpais.es Online edition of Spain's biggest-selling non-sports daily paper. English edition available.

www.feve.es Website of the coastal FEVE train service.

www.guiarepsol.com Excellent online route planner for Spanish roads, also available in English.

www.idealspain.com A good source of practical information about the country designed for people relocating there.

www.inm.es Site of the national metereological institute, with the day's weather and next-day forecasts.

www.movelia.es Online timetables and ticketing for several bus companies.

www.paginasamarillas.es Yellow Pages.

www.paginasblancas.es The White Pages.

www.parador.es Parador information, including locations, prices and photos.

www.red2000.com A good introduction to Spanish geography and culture, with listings.

www.renfe.es Online timetables and tickets for RENFE train network.

www.soccer-spain.com A website in English dedicated to Spanish football.

www.spain.info The official website of the Spanish tourist board.

www.ticketmaster.es Spain's biggest ticketing agency for concerts, etc, with online purchase.

www.todoturismorural.com and **www.toprural.com** 2 excellent sites for *casas rurales*.

www.tourspain.es A useful website run by the Spanish tourist board.

www.typicallyspanish.com News and links on all things Spanish.

Visas

Entry requirements are subject to change, so always check with the Spanish tourist board or an embassy/consulate if you're not an EU citizen. EU citizens and those from countries within the Schengen agreement can enter Spain freely. UK/Irish citizens will need to carry a passport, while an identity card suffices for other EU/Schengen nationals. Citizens of Australia, the USA, Canada, New Zealand and Israel can enter without a visa for up to 90 days. Other citizens will require a visa, obtainable from Spanish consulates or embassies. These are usually issued very quickly and valid for all Schengen countries. The basic visa is valid for 90 days, and you'll need 2 passport photos, proof of funds covering your stay and possibly evidence of medical cover (ie insurance). For extensions of visas, apply to an *oficina de extranjeros* in a major city.

Contents

Footprint features

Bilbao & Basque Region

Bilbao/Bilbo

In an amazingly short time, and without losing sight of its roots, Bilbao, the dirty industrial city, has successfully transformed itself into a buzzing cultural capital. The Guggenheim museum is the undoubted flagship of this triumphant progress, a sinuous fantasy of a building that will take your breath away. It inspires because of what it is, but also because the city had the vision to build it. While the museum has led the turnaround, much of what is enjoyable about modern Bilbao was already there. Bustling bar-life, harmonious old and new architecture, a superb eating culture, and a tangible sense of pride in being a working city are still things that make Bilbao special, and the exciting new developments have only added to those qualities.

The Casco Viejo, the old town, still evokes a cramped medieval past. Along its web of attractive streets, designer clothing stores occupy the ground floors where families perhaps once huddled behind the city walls. El Ensanche, the new town, has an elegant European feel to it. The wealth of the city is more evident here, with stately banks and classy shops lining the planned avenues. The riverbank is the most obvious beneficiary of Bilbao's leap into the 21st century: Calatrava's eerily skeletal bridge, designer promenades and Gehry's exuberant Guggenheim bring art and architecture together and make the Río Nervión the city's axis once more. It doesn't stop there, as ongoing work is further softening the remaining industrial edges.

The seaside suburbs, once reached by hours of painstaking river navigation, are now a nonchalant 20 minutes away by metro. Fashionable Getxo has a relaxed beach atmosphere, while, across the estuary, Portugalete still seems to be wondering how Bilbao gets all the credit these days: for hundreds of years it was a far more important port. ▸ *For listings, see pages 38-49.*

Ins and outs

Getting there Bilbao's airport is one of two international ones in Euskadi, and is a good gateway to Northern Spain with connections to several European destinations. The Portsmouth–Bilbao ferry service is no longer operational. The city is well served by buses from the rest of the nation and is exceedingly well connected with Vitoria, San Sebastián and smaller destinations in Euskadi. There are a few train services to other Spanish cities and a narrow-gauge line along the coast to Santander, Oviedo and Galicia. ▶▶ *See Transport, page 48.*

Getting around Central Bilbao isn't too large and is reasonably walkable. The Guggenheim museum, as far afield as many people get, is about 20 minutes' walk from the old town along the river. For farther-flung parts of Bilbao, such as the beach or the bus station, the metro is excellent. Sir Norman Foster's design is simple, attractive and, above all, spacious. Although there's a reasonable network of local bus services in Bilbao, they are only generally useful for a handful of destinations; these are indicated in the text. The newly re-established tram network is handy, particularly for reaching the Guggenheim from the old town. There's just one line so far; a scenic one, running from Atxuri station along the river, skirting the Casco Viejo (stopping behind the Teatro Arriaga), then continuing on the other side of the Nervión, stopping at the Guggenheim and the bus station among other places.

Best time to visit Bilbao's summers are warm but not baking. This is the best time to visit, but be sure to book ahead during the boisterous August fiesta (see Festivals and events, page 47). At other times of year, Bilbao is a fairly wet place, but never gets especially cold. The bar life and museums provide ample distraction from the drizzle.

Tourist information Bilbao's main **tourist office** ① *Plaza Arriaga s/n, T944 795 760, bit@ ayto.bilbao.net, Mon-Fri 1100-1400, 1700-1930, Sat 0930-1400, 1700-1930, Sun 0930-1400,* has temporarily moved to the Teatro Arriaga on the edge of the old town. There's another in the **new town** ① *Plaza Ensanche 11, Mon-Fri 0900-1400, 1600-1930.* There is also a smaller office by the **Guggenheim museum** ① *Abandoibarra Etorbidea 2, Tue-Fri 1100-1800, Sat 1100-1900, Sun 1100-1700,* and an office at the airport. There's also a **tourist information line** ① *T944 710 301, operational daily 0830-2300.* The offices can provide a good free map of the city; they can also sell you the **Bilbao Card**, which allows free transport on local buses, metro, tram and the Artxanda funicular, as well as providing discounts in several shops and museums. It costs €6 for a day, €10 for two days, or €12 for three days. Make sure you also pick up a copy of the excellent bi-monthly tourist magazine *Bilbao Guía.* The city's website, www.bilbao.net, is also a good source of information. The tourist board also runs an accommodation and event-booking website, www.bilbaoreservas.com, T902 877 298.

Background

In 1300 the lord of the province of Vizcaya, Don Diego López de Haro V, saw the potential of the riverside fishing village of Bilbao and granted it permission to become a town. The people graciously accepted, and by the end of the 14th century history records that the town had three parallel streets: Somera, Artekale and Tendería. These were soon added to: Belostikale, Carnicería Vieja, Barrenkale and Barrenkale Barrena, forming the Siete Calles – the seven original streets of the city. It was a time of much strife and the fledgling town was walled, but at the end of the 15th century these original fortifications came down and the city began to grow.

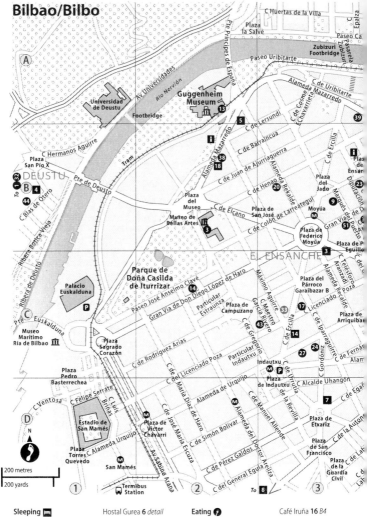

Bilbao/Bilbo

Sleeping 🛏	Hostal Gurea 6 *detail*	Eating 🍴	Café Iruña 16 *B4*
Albergue Bilbao	Hostal Mardones 10 *detail*	Arbola Gaña 3 *B2*	Café La Granja 52 *B4*
Aterpetxea 8 *D3*	Hostal Méndez 11 *detail*	Artajo 2 *B4*	Café Lamiak 22 *detail*
Apartamentos Atxuri 19 *C6*	Indautxu 7 *D3*	Asador Ibáñez	Capuccino 24 *C3*
Arriaga 1 *detail*	Iturrienea Ostatua 17 *detail*	de Bilbao 5 *A4*	Casa Vasca 32 *B1*
Carlton 3 *B3*	Miróhotel Bilbao 18 *B2*	Asian Chic 21 *B4*	Colmado Ibérico 7 *C4*
Deusto 4 *B1*	Pensión Ladero 16 *detail*	Bar Irintzi 15 *detail*	Egiluz 25 *detail*
Ercilla 14 *C3*	Pensión Manoli 9 *detail*	Berton 4 *detail*	El Globo 35 *B3*
Gran Domine Bilbao 5 *A2*	Petit Palace Arana 13 *detail*	Boulevard 8 *detail*	El Kiosko del Arenal 10 *A5*
Hostal Begoña 2 *B4*	Sirimiri 12 *B6*	Café-Bar Bilbao 6 *detail*	Garibolo 11 *C4*

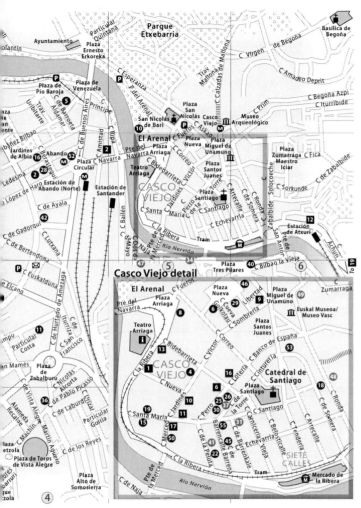

Casco Viejo detail

			Bars & clubs
Gatz **12** *detail*	Lekeitio **23** *B3*	Serantes II **27** *C3*	Bizitza **37** *detail*
Guggenheim **13** *A2*	Mina **40** *C6*	Serantes III **38** *B2*	Bullitt Groove Club **47** *C5*
Guria **14** *C2*	Mr Lee **36** *D4*	Su@ **9** *B3*	Compañía del Ron **33** *C3*
Hostaria Marchese del	New Inn **42** *B4*	Taberna Taurina **28** *B4*	Conjunto Vacío **34** *B5*
Porto **51** *B3*	Okela **43** *C3*	Taloaska **1** *B1*	Errondabide **48** *detail*
Jaunak **18** *detail*	Oriotarra **44** *B1*	Urkia **53** *detail*	Luz Gas **41** *detail*
Kasko **19** *detail*	Río Oja **25** *detail*	Victor **29** *detail*	Muga **49** *detail*
Kuku Soak **55** *detail*	Rotterdam **26** *detail*	Víctor Montes **46** *detail*	Zulo **31** *detail*
Laga **50** *detail*	Saibigain **45** *detail*	Xukela **30** *detail*	
La Viña **20** *B3*	Serantes **17** *C3*	Zortziko **39** *A3*	

Bilbao suffered during the first Carlist war in the 19th century, when the liberal city was besieged (ultimately unsuccessfully) by the reactionary Carlist forces. The one bright spot to emerge was the invention of *bacalao al pil-pil*, now the city's signature dish, but originally devised due to lack of any fresh produce to eat. Not long after the war, Bilbao's boom started. The Vizcayan hills harboured huge reserves of haematite, the ore from which the city's iron was produced. By the middle of the century, it had become evident that this was by far the best ore for the new process of steelmaking. Massive foreign investment followed, particularly from Britain, and the city expanded rapidly as workers flooded in from all parts of the peninsula. The good times didn't last, however, and by the early 20th century things were looking grimmer. Output declined and dissatisfied workers sank into poverty. The Civil War hit the city hard too; after the Republican surrender, Franco made it clear he wasn't prepared to forgive the Basques for siding against him. Repressed and impoverished, the great industrial success story of the late 19th century fell into gloom. The dictator's death sparked a massive reflowering of Basque culture, symbolized by the bold steps taken to revitalize the city. The Guggenheim's opening in 1997 confirmed Bilbao as a cultural capital of Northern Spain, and ongoing regeneration works proceed apace.

Casco Viejo

Bilbao's old town is a good place to start exploring the city. This is where most of the budget accommodation and bar life is based. Tucked into a bend in the river, it's the most charming part of town, a lively jumble of pedestrian streets that has always been the city's social focus. There's something of the medina about it; on your first few forays you surely won't end up where you might have thought you were going.

Siete Calles
The parallel Siete Calles (seven streets) are the oldest part of town, and even locals struggle to sort out which bar is on which street. While there aren't a huge number of sights per se, there are dozens of quirky shops and some very attractive architecture; leisurely wandering is in order. The true soul of the Casco emerges from early evening on, however, when Bilbaínos descend like bees returning to the hive, strolling the streets, listening to buskers, debating the quality of the *pintxos* in the myriad bars and sipping wine in the setting sun.

Catedral de Santiago
In the centre of the old town area is the **Catedral de Santiago** ① *Tue-Sat 1000-1300, 1600-1900, Sun 1030-1330, free*, whose slender spire rises high above the tight streets. A graceful Gothic affair, it was mostly built in the late 14th century on the site of a previous church, but was devastated by fire in the 1500s and lost much of its original character. Two of its best features are later additions: an arched southern porch and a small but harmonious cloister (if it's locked, ask an attendant). The interior is small and has an inclusive, democratic air. Also worth spotting is a beautifully worked Gothic tomb in the chapel of San Antón. Promoted to cathedral in 1950, the building has benefited from recent restoration work. A few shops are charmingly nestled into its flank.

Plaza Nueva
The 'New Square', one of a series of similar cloister-like squares in Euskadi, was finished in 1849. Described by Unamuno (see box, page 120) as "my cold and uniform Plaza

Nueva", it will particularly appeal to lovers of geometry and symmetry with its courtly neoclassical arches, which conceal an excellent selection of restaurants and bars, offering some of the best *pintxos* in town. In good weather, most have seating outside in the square.

Museo Vasco

Near the Plaza Nueva, the **Euskal Museoa/Museo Vasco** ① *Plaza Miguel de Unamuno 4, T944 155 423, www.euskal-museoa.org, Tue-Sat 1100-1700, Sun 1100-1400, €3 (free on Thu)*, is attractively set around an old Jesuit college and houses an interesting if higgledy-piggledy series of Basque artefacts and exhibits covering thousands of years. There's a fascinating room-sized relief model of Vizcaya on the top floor, a piece of one of the Gernika oak trees and some good displays on Basque fishing. Across the square and up the steps, the new **Museo Arqueológico** ① *Calzadas de Mallona 2, T944 040 990, Tue-Sat 1000-1400, 1600-1930, Sun 1030-1400, €3*, has a well-presented overview of Vizcaya's prehistory and history through material finds. Most of the prehistoric artefacts were found in caves around the province.

Arenal and around

Formerly an area of marshy sand, the Arenal was drained in the 18th century. It is now a busy nexus point for strollers, lovers, demonstrators and dog walkers, and has a bandstand with frequent performances, often of folk dancing. Next to it is the 18th-century baroque façade of **San Nicolás de Bari**. Opposite, the **Teatro Arriaga** seems very sure of itself these days, but was only reopened in 1986 after decades of neglect. It's very much in plush *fin de siècle* theatre style, with chandeliers, soft carpet and sweeping staircases, but at times presents some fairly cutting-edge art, usually of a strong standard and fairly priced.

Basílica de Begoña

Atop a steep hill above the Casco Viejo, the Basílica de Begoña is Bilbao's most important church, home of the Virgin of Begoña, the patron of Vizcaya. It's built in Gothic style on the site of a chapel where the Virgin is said to have appeared in former times. The cloister is a later addition, as is the flamboyant tower, which gives a slightly unbalanced feel to the building. To get there from the Casco Viejo, take the lift from Calle Esperanza or leave the metro station by the 'Begoña/Mallona' exit. From there, walk up the hill to the basilica. Buses No 3 and No 30 come here from Plaza Circular, or bus No 41 from Gran Vía. On your way back down, rather than taking the Mallona lift, head down the flight of stairs next to it; a charming descent into the Casco Viejo warren, emerging on Plaza Unamuno.

Along the riverbank

"You are, Nervión, the history of the town, you are her past and her future, you are memory always becoming hope." Miguel de Unamuno.

The **Nervión** made Bilbao and Bilbao almost killed the Nervión; until recently pollution levels were sky-high. Although your immune system would still have words to say about taking a dip, the change is noticeable. The riverbank has been and continues to be the focus of most of Bilbao's beautification schemes; if you only take one stroll in Bilbao, an evening *paseo* from the Casco Viejo along the river to the Guggenheim should be it.

Cross the river at the **Zubizuri** footbridge, one of the most graceful of the acclaimed bridges of Santiago Calatrava. After crossing the footbridge, you are on the **Paseo Uribitarte**; this riverside walk leading to the Guggenheim museum is where plenty of Bilbaínos gather for the evening stroll.

The tram is a good way to see the river, running more or less along it from Atxuri station to the Guggenheim and Euskalduna palace.

Museo Guggenheim

ⓘ *Abandoibarra Etorbidea 2, T944 359 000, www.guggenheim-bilbao.es, Tue-Sun 1000-2000 (Jul and Aug daily 1000-2000), €13 including audio guide, students/pensioners €7.50, children under 12 free, €13.50 including Museo de Bellas Artes; guided tours free at 1130, 1230, 1630, 1830 (Spanish, English and Euskara).*

Daring in concept and brilliant in execution, the Guggenheim museum has driven a boom in the local confidence as well as, more prosaically, the economy; its success gave the green light to further ambitious transformations of the formerly industrialized parts of the city.

It all started when the Guggenheim Foundation decided to build a new museum to enable more of their collection to be exhibited. Many cities around the globe were considered, but Bilbao was keenest and the Basque government were prepared to foot the US$100 million bill for its construction.

Frank Gehry was the man who won the design competition and the rest is the reality of what confronts visitors to Bilbao today: a shining temple of a building that completely fulfils the maxim of 'architecture as art'. Gehry's masterstroke was to use titanium, an expensive soft metal normally reserved for Boeing aircraft and the like. He was intrigued by its futuristic sheen and malleable qualities; the panels are literally paper-thin. The titanium makes the building shimmer: it seems that the architect has managed to capture motion.

One of the most impressive features of the design is the way it interacts with the city. One of Bilbao's enjoyable and surprising experiences is to look up when crossing a street in the centre of town and see the Guggenheim perfectly framed, like some unearthly craft that's just landed. Gehry had to contend with the ugly bulk of the Puente de la Salve running through the middle of his site, yet managed to incorporate the bridge fluidly into his plans. The raised tower at the museum's eastern end has no architectural purpose other than to link the building more effectively with the town upriver; it works.

The building also interacts fluidly with the river itself; the pool at the museum's feet almost seems part of the Nervión, and Fuyiko Nakaya's mist sculpture, when turned on, further blurs things. It's entitled *FOG*, which also happen to be the architect's initials. The same pool also hosts Yves Klein's Fire Fountain pyrotechnics.

A couple of creatures have escaped the confines of the gallery and sit in the open air. Jeff Koons's giant floral sculpture, *Puppy*, sits eagerly greeting visitors. Formerly a touring attraction visiting the city for the opening of the museum in 1997, he couldn't escape the clutches of the kitsch-hungry Bilbaínos, who demanded that he stayed put. On the other side of the building, a sinister spider-like creature guards the waterside approach. Entitled *Maman*, we can only be thankful that late sculptor Louise Bourgeois's mother had long since passed away when it was created. It's a striking piece of work, and makes a bizarre sight if approached when the mist is on. More comforting are Koons's colourful bunch of *Tulips* by the pool under the gallery's eaves.

So much for the exterior, which has met with worldwide acclaim. What about the inside? It is, after all, an art museum. Gehry's idea was that there would be two types of gallery within the building: "galleries for dead artists, which have classical square or rectangular shapes,

The philosopher's last stand

One of Bilbao's most famous sons was Miguel de Unamuno, poet, philosopher and academic, born in 1864 on Calle Ronda. A member of the 'Generation of '98' – a new wave of artists and thinkers emerging in the wake of the Spanish-American war of 1898 – Unamuno, who spoke 15 languages, was a humanist and a Catholic with an idealistic love of truth. This made him enemies in a Spain where political beliefs tended to come first. To this day, many Basques have mixed feelings about 'Don Miguel', who, although proud of being Basque, wasn't pro-independence and deplored some of the myths created in the name of nationalism.

Unamuno became rector of the university at Salamanca but after criticizing the dictatorship of Primo de Rivera, he was imprisoned in the Canary Islands, from where his rescue was organized by the editor of the French newspaper *Le Quotidien*.

In Salamanca when the Civil War broke out, Unamuno, previously a deputy in the Republic, had supported the rising, but grew more and more alarmed with the nature of the Nationalist movement and the character of the war. On 12 October, 1936 he was presiding over the Columbus day ceremony at the university. The gathering degenerated into a fascist propaganda session. Catalan nationalism was denounced as a cancer that fascism would cut out, and General Millán Astray, a war veteran, continued with more empty rhetoric; the hall resounded to the popular Falangist slogan "Viva la muerte", or "long live death".

Unamuno rose to close the meeting: "At times to be silent is to lie", he said, and went on to criticize harshly what had been said. The general responded by crying "Death to intellectuals". Guns were pointed at the 72-year-old, who continued: "You will win, because you have the brute force. But you will not convince. For to convince, you would need what you lack: reason and right in the struggle". At the end of his speech, he was ushered out of the tumultuous hall by Franco's wife to safety. Under house arrest, he died a couple of months later, it was said, of a broken heart. On the day of his death, his two sons enlisted in the anti-fascist militia.

and galleries for living artists, which have funny shapes, because they can fight back". The embodiment of the latter is the massive Gallery 104, built with the realization that many modern artworks are too big for traditional museums. This has been dedicated to Richard Serra's magnificent *The Matter of Time*, an installation now consisting of eight monumental structures of curved oxidised steel centered around *Snake*, whose curved sheets will carry whispers from one end to another. A hundred feet long, and weighing 180 tons, it's meant to be interactive – walk through it, talk through it, touch it. Other pieces, including one that's disturbingly maze-like, play with space, angles, and perception in different ways. Off the gallery is an interpretative exhibition on the pieces. This, however, is one of only a few pieces that live in the museum; the rest are temporary visitors, some taken from the permanent collection of the Guggenheim Foundation, others appearing in a range of exhibitions. This, of course, means that the overall quality varies according to what's on show.

Architecturally, the interior is a very soothing space, with natural light flooding into the atrium. It's a relief to realize that this isn't one of those galleries that makes you feel you'll never be able to see everything unless you rush about; it's very uncluttered and manageable. In the atrium is Jenny Holzer's accurately titled *Installation for Bilbao*, an arresting nine-column LED display that unites the different levels of the building. The effect created is a torrent of primal human sentiment expressed simply in three languages. Nearby are Jim Dine's towering but headless *Three Red Spanish Venuses*.

There are three floors of galleries devoted to temporary exhibitions radiating off the central space. For a look at some smaller-scale Frank Gehry work, drop into the reading room on the ground floor, furnished with his unusual cardboard chairs and tables, which are surprisingly comfortable and solid. The cafés also feature chairs designed by him. As well as the usual gallery shop, the museum also has an excellent modern art bookshop.

The closest metro stop to the museum is Moyúa, but it's a few blocks away; better is the tram, which stops just outside.

There's a spot in the museum designed to display Picasso's *Gernika*, which the Basque government persistently try to prise away from the Reina Sofía gallery in Madrid.

Palacio Euskalduna
Beyond the Guggenheim, the Euskalduna Palace is a bizarre modern building that echoes both the shipbuilding industry and Vizcaya's iron trade. It's now a major venue for conferences and concerts, particularly classical. More *simpático* is the covered Euskalduna bridge nearby, which sweeps into Deustu in a confident curve.

Museo Marítimo Ría de Bilbao
ⓘ *Muelle Ramón de la Sota 1, T902 131 000, www.museomaritimobilbao.org, Tue-Fri 1000-1800 (2000 summer), Sat and Sun 1000-2000, €5 (extra applies for special exhibitions).*
This newish museum nestles under the Euskalduna bridge and examines the maritime history of this proud city. It's on the site of what was once an important shipbuilding and cargo area; a massive derrick and various ships in dry dock are part of the exterior exhibition. Inside, the focus is on the Bilbao estuary and Vizcayan shipping in general. It's dry but fascinating, with a couple of good AV presentations in English (other displays have translation sheets). One of the highlights is the aerial photograph of Bilbao and its *ría*. There are often excellent temporary exhibitions, which have included visiting 'guest ships' that moor outside.

Deustu

Across from the Guggenheim is Deusto (recently officially renamed Deustu), a bohemian university district buzzing with purpose. Sometimes dubbed 'The Republic of Deusto', it developed separately from Bilbao for much of its history and still has a different vibe. Traditionally frequented by artists, students and agitators, the cafés and bars hum with political discussion. If you want that perfect snap of Frank Gehry's masterpiece, this is the place to come, particularly in the evening light.

The Universidad de Deustu, Bilbao's main university, was founded in 1886 by the Jesuits. It now counts over 20,000 students and staff among its several buildings. While the academic standard of the university has traditionally been very high, it was an important centre of radical opposition to the Franco dictatorship, and has also played an important role in Basque nationalism.

On Deustu's waterfront, a large sculptured stone feline defies the sky. This building was originally a pavilion to house the small workshops of local tradespeople but has now been converted into luxury apartments. Bilbaínos call it **El Tigre** (the tiger), but the city is divided; many agree that it's actually a lioness.

El Ensanche

The residents of old Bilbao had long been crammed into the small Casco Viejo area when the boom came and the population began to surge. In 1876 the Plan de Ensanche (expansion) de Bilbao was approved, and the area across the river was drawn up into segments governed by the curve of the Nervión. The Ensanche quickly became Bilbao's business district, and it remains so today, its graceful avenues lined with stately buildings, prestige shops and numerous bars.

Museo de Bellas Artes

ⓘ *Plaza del Museo 2, T944 396 060, www.museobilbao.com, Metro Moyúa, Tue-Sun 1000-2000, €6, free Wed, €13.50 with Guggenheim, €2 audio guide.*

Not to be outdone by its titanium colleague, the fine arts museum has tried to keep up with the times by adding a modern building of its own on to the existing museum. The result is a harmonious credit to its architect, Luis Uriarte, who seamlessly and attractively fused new to old. Similarly, the collection is a medley of modern (mostly Basque) art and older works – there's also a new space for temporary exhibitions.

The Basque sculptors Eduardo Chillida and Jorge de Oteiza (see box, page 55) are both well represented, but the museum confidently displays more avant-garde multimedia work by young artists too. Among the portraits, the jutting jaw of the Habsburg kings is visible in two famous works. The first, of a young Felipe II, is by the Dutchman Moro, while the Felipe IV, attributed to Velásquez, and similar to his portrait of the same king in the Prado, is a master work. The decline of Spain can be seen in the sad king's haunted but intelligent eyes, which seem to follow the viewer around the room. A lighter note is perhaps unintentionally struck by the anonymous *Temptations of St Anthony*, who is pestered by a trio of colourful demons. Among other items of interest is a painting of Bilbao by Paret y Alcázar. Dating from 1793 and painted from the Arenal, it looks like a sleepy riverside village. Here too, is a very good modern restaurant upstairs offering great views.

Plaza de Toros de Vista Alegre

ⓘ *Check the website, www.plazatorosbilbao.com, for details of corridas and ticketing.*

Bilbao's temple of bullfighting sees most action during *Semana Grande* in August, when there are *corridas* all week. The locals are knowledgeable and demanding of their matadors, and the bulls they face are acknowledged to be among the most *bravo* in Spain. Tickets to the spectacles don't come cheap, starting at about €30. The bullring is also home to a **museum** ⓘ *C Martín Agüero 1, T944 448 698, Metro Indautxu, Mon-Fri 1030-1300, 1600-1800, €3*, dedicated to tauromachy. There are displays on the history of the practice, as well as memorabilia of famous matadors and bulls.

Estadio de San Mamés

ⓘ *C Felipe Serrate s/n, Metro San Mamés, T944 411 445, www.athletic-club.net.*

The Estadio de San Mamés is at the far end of the new town. Few in the world are the football teams with the social and political significance of Athletic Bilbao (see box, page 124); support of the team is a religion, and this, their home stadium, is known as the Cathedral of Football. Services are held fortnightly, usually on Sundays at 1700. The Basque crowd are fervent but good-natured. It's well worth going to a game; it's a far more friendly and social scene than the average match in the rest of Europe. The Monday papers frequently devote 10 pages or more to Athletic's game. Tickets usually go on sale at the ground two days

Athletic Bilbao

Rarely is a football team loved quite as deeply as Athletic Club are by Bilbao. A Basque symbol in the same league as the *ikurriña* or the Gernika oak, the team, as a matter of principle, only fields Basque players. Astonishingly they have remained competitive in one of the strongest leagues in the world and have never been relegated. To date, they have won the championship eight times (more than any other club bar the two Madrid giants and Barcelona) and have won 24 Spanish Cups.

Athletic Club grew out of the cultural exchange that was taking place in the late 19th century between Bilbao and the UK. British workers brought football to Bilbao, and Basques went to Britain to study engineering. In the early years, Athletic fielded many British players, and their strip was modelled on that of Sunderland, where many of the miners were from. José Antonio Aguirre, who led the Civil War Basque government so nobly, had been a popular player up front for the club.

before the game. On match days, the ticket office opens two hours before kick-off. Tickets range from €25-50 depending on location. The ground also holds a small **museum** ① *Tue-Sat 1000-1400, 1600-1900 (1830 winter), Sun 1000-1400, €6*, displaying trophies and other memorabilia of 'Los Leones'. Entry includes a guided tour of the stadium.

Bilbao's seafront → *For listings, see pages 38-49.*

At the mouth of the estuary of the Nervión, around 20 km from Bilbao, the fashionable barrio of Getxo is linked by the improbably massive Puente Vizcaya with the grittier town of Portugalete, in its day a flourishing medieval port. It's a great day trip from Bilbao; the fresh air here is a treat for tired lungs, and not far from Getxo stretch the languid beach suburbs of Sopelana, Plentzia and Gorliz.

Getxo

Very much a separate town rather than a suburb of Bilbao, Getxo is a wealthy, sprawling district encompassing the eastern side of the river mouth, a couple of beaches, a modern marina, and a petite old harbour. It's home to a good set of attractive stately mansions as well as a tiny but oh-so-pretty whitewashed old village around the now disused fishing port-ette. There's a very relaxed feel about the place, perhaps born from a combination of the seaside air and a lack of anxiety about where the next meal is coming from.

The **Playa de Ereaga** is Getxo's principal stretch of sand, and location of its **tourist office** ① *T944 910 800*, and finer hotels. Near it, the **Puerto Viejo** is a tiny harbour, now silted up, and a reminder of the days when Getxo made its living from fish. The solemn statues of a fisherman and a *sardinera* stand on the stairs that look over it, perhaps mystified at the lack of boats. Perching above, a densely packed knot of white houses and narrow lanes gives the little village a very Mediterranean feel – unless the *sirimiri*, the Bilbao drizzle, has put in an appearance. There are a couple of restaurants and bars to soak up the ambience of this area, which is Getxo's prettiest quarter.

Further around, the **Playa de Arrigunaga** is a better beach flanked by crumbly cliffs, one topped by a windmill, which some days has a better time of it than the shivering bathers. A pleasant, if longish, walk leads downhill to the estuary end of Getxo, past the marina, and an ostentatious series of 20th-century *palacios* on the waterfront, and a

La Pasionaria

"It is better to be the widow of a hero than the wife of a coward." Dolores Ibárruri.

One of the most prominent figures of the Spanish Civil War, Dolores Ibárruri, from the Bilbao suburb of Gallarta, near Portugalete, was known as La Pasionaria (the passion flower) for her inspirational public speaking.

Formerly a servant and a *sardinera* (sardine seller), she suffered grinding poverty and the loss of two daughters in infancy, but rose to prominence in the Communist Party in the 1930s, becoming a deputy in the parliament in 1936 (she was released from prison to take up her post). When the Civil War broke out, she became a powerful symbol of the defence of Madrid and the struggle against fascism as well as empowered womanhood. Straightforward, determined and always dressed in black, she adopted the war cry *"No pasarán"* (they shall not pass), which

was taken up all over Republican Spain. She was instrumental in the recruitment and morale of anti-fascist soldiers, including the International Brigades. When the latter were withdrawn, she famously thanked them: "You can go proudly. You are history. You are legend … We shall not forget you". Ibárruri was never much involved in the plotting and infighting that plagued the Republican cause and was able to claim at the end of the war: "I have neither blood nor gold upon my hands". When Franco was victorious in 1939, she flew to Russia, where she lived in Moscow. The dictator died in 1975 and, after 38 years, Ibárruri was re-elected to her old seat at the first elections in 1977. On her return to Spain the 82-year-old Pasionaria, still in black, proclaimed to a massive crowd: "I said they shall not pass, and they haven't". She died in 1989.

monument to Churruca, whose engineering made the estuary navigable, making Bilbao accessible to large vessels; a vital step in its growth.

Passing the hulking modern **Iglesia de Nuestra Señora de las Mercedes** (which contains some highly regarded frescoes) will bring you to the unmistakable form of the Puente Vizcaya and the trendy shopping area of **Las Arenas** (Areeta).

Puente Vizcaya

ⓘ *www.puente-colgante.com, 1000-2200 crossings, 1000-dusk walkway; crossings €0.30 per person, €1.10 per car; walkway €5, Metro Areeta or Portugalete.*

A bizarre cross between a bridge and a ferry, the Puente Vizcaya was opened in 1893, a time when large steel structures were à la mode in Europe. Wanting to connect the estuary towns of Getxo and Portugalete by road, but not wanting a bridge that would block the *ría* to shipping, the solution taken was to use a 'gondola' suspended by cables from a high steel span. It's a fascinating piece of engineering: the modern gondola fairly zooms back and forth with six cars plus foot passengers aboard. You can also ascend to the walkway 50 m above. You'll often see the bridge referred to as the **Puente Colgante** (hanging bridge).

Portugalete

On the other side of the Puente Vizcaya from Getxo is Portugalete, a solid working-class seamen's town with a significant seafaring history. In former times, before Churruca did his channelling work, the Nervión estuary was a silty minefield of shoals, meanders and sandbars – a nightmare to navigate in anything larger than a rowing boat. Thus Bilbao was still a good few hours' journey by boat, and Portugalete's situation at the mouth of the *ría* gave it great importance as a port. Nowadays, although from across the water it looks thoroughly functional, it preserves a characterful old town and attractive waterfront promenade.

Above the waterside the old Casco is dominated by the **Iglesia de Santa María**, commissioned by Doña María the Kind at the time of the town's beginnings, although the current building, in Gothic style, dates from the early 16th century. There's a small museum inside. Next to it, the **Torre de Salazar** is what remains of the formidable compound built by Juan López de Salazar, a major landowner, in about 1380. The main living area was originally on the second floor – the first was a prison – and the tower was occupied until 1934, when a fire evicted the last residents. A member of the Salazar family who lived here, Luis García, was one of the first chroniclers of Vizcaya. He had plenty of time to devote to his writings, as he spent the last few years of his life locked up by his loving sons. For **tourist information** ① *T944 958 741, turismo@portugalete.org.*

Bilbao/Bilbo listings

For Sleeping and Eating price codes and other relevant information, see pages 12-19.

🛏 Sleeping

Bilbao *p26, map p28*
Finding accommodation is frequently difficult; it's worth phoning ahead, although some of the *pensiones* won't take reservations. Most budget accommodation is in or near the Casco Viejo, while the classier hotels are spread through the new town.
€€€€ Gran Domine Bilbao, Alameda Mazarredo 61, T944 253 300, www. granhoteldomine bilbao.com. This modern 5-star hotel is directly opposite the Guggenheim and has been designed with the same innovation and levity in mind. The original façade of the building consists of 48 mirrors at slightly different angles, while the delightful interior is dominated by a large central atrium. The rooms with Guggenheim views cost a little more, but it's worth it when you're paying prices of this level (though online discounts are plentiful outside peak times). There's also a good bar and restaurant. Inspiringly original. Recommended.
€€€€ Hotel Carlton, Plaza Moyúa 2, T944 162 200, www.hotelcarlton.es. This grand old hotel, set on noisy Plaza Moyúa, is considerably more luxurious inside than out. Its refurbished neoclassical ambience has colonnaded Einstein, Lorca and Hemingway, among other

notables. Rooms are spacious, and there are some very interesting prices online.
€€€€ Hotel Ercilla, C Ercilla 37-39, T944 705 700, www.hotelercilla.es. Well located on the city's main shopping street, this large 4-star hotel has a cheerful entrance. It's newly renovated and is much the better for it. With quality service and a busy, metropolitan feel, it makes a convenient base, and is well priced for the amenities on offer. There are excellent weekend rates, with savings of up to 40%. Check the website for current offers.
€€€ Hotel Indautxu, Plaza Bombero Etxaniz s/n, T944 211 198, www.hotelindautxu. com. Behind a mirrored façade that bizarrely dwarfs the older building in front, are comfortable executive-style rooms, set on a comparatively quiet square. There's a terrace, and pianists make the occasional scheduled appearance in the bar. More character than many in this category and cheerful to boot.
€€€ Miróhotel Bilbao, Alameda Mazarredo 77, T946 611 880, www.mirohotelbilbao. com. Also close to the Guggenheim, with some great views of it, this is a sleek hotel with a Catalan touch; both architect Carmen Abad and interior designer Antonio Miró hail from Barcelona. It's impressively modern, with a pared-back feel not without touches of whimsy. The rooms are excellent: spacious and with a Nordic feel to the white fittings. Rates vary substantially according to when you reserve; you may get better deals from

an online broker or travel agent than the hotel's own website. There are all services, including an enjoyable jacuzzi and a stylish bar. Staff are helpful and friendly.

€€€ Hotel Deustu, C Francisco Maciá 9, T944 760 006, www.nhhoteles.com, Metro Deustu. This colourfully decorated hotel is an enjoyable place to stay on this side of the river. The large rooms, featuring minibar, safe, PlayStation and inviting beds are offset by an attractively arty bar and restaurant downstairs. Extras like internet are immodestly expensive though.

€€€ Petit Palace Arana, C Bidebarrieta 2, T944 156 411, www.hthoteles.com. With an unbeatable location at the mouth of the warren that is the Casco Viejo, this beautiful building has been very sensitively converted into a smart modern hotel. There's free Internet access for guests, and the best of the rooms have a computer terminal and exercise bike. There are innovative family suites with fold-down beds (good value), a pretty upstairs breakfast room, and rooms equipped for the disabled. Book on the internet in advance for the best rates. The closest parking is the Arenal.

€€ Apartamentos Atxuri, Av Miraflores 17, T944 667 832, www.apartamentosatxuri. com. These beautifully sleek apartments occupy a modern building a 5-min walk east of the Casco Viejo and not far from the Atxuri terminus of the tram. Spacious, spotless, and decorated with style, they have either 1 or 2 double rooms as well as a sofa-bed in the lounge. Staff are helpful and facilities excellent.

€€ Hotel Arriaga, C Ribera 3, T944 790 001, www.hotelarriaga.es. Very friendly hotel with a garage (rare in the Casco Viejo) and some excellent rooms with floor-to-ceiling windows and views over the theatre. Plush, formal-style decoration and fittings, a bit old-fashioned but with plenty of charm. Free Wi-Fi. Good value.

€€ Hotel Sirimiri, Plaza de la Encarnación 3, T944 330 759, www.hotelsirimiri.com. Named after the light misty rain that is a feature of the city, this is a small gem of a hotel in a quiet square a short stroll from the Casco Viejo. The genial owner has equipped it with a gym and sauna, and there's limited free parking – a big saving – at the back. Rooms come with heating but not a/c. The twins are much more spacious than some of the doubles. Follow signs for Miraflores/Atxuri from the motorway and it's very easily reached. Recommended.

€€ Hostal Begoña, C Amistad 2, T944 230 134, www.actioturis.com. Very handy for the train station and Casco Viejo, this is a welcoming modern hotel packed with flair and comfort. From the inviting library/lounge to the large chalet-style rooms and mini-suites at very reasonable prices, this is an excellent option. The hotel also offers free internet access and Wi-Fi, and can organize a range of outdoor activities. **Pensión Bilbao** in the same building is a more than acceptable fallback if the **Begoña** is full. Highly recommended.

€€ Hostal Gurea, C Bidebarrieta 14, T944 163 299, www.hostalgureabilbao.com. Carefully refurbished and well-scrubbed establishment on one of the Casco Viejo's principal axes. Welcoming and cheerfully vague about bookings. Rooms are all en suite and comfortable if by no means luxurious. Free Wi-Fi.

€€ Hostal Mardones, C Jardines 4, T944 153 105, www.hostalmardones.com. Run by a welcoming and chatty owner and very well situated in *pintxo* heartland. Entered by the side of a newsstand, the *pensión* is fitted in attractive dark wood, and rooms are pleasant, light and airy. There's free Wi-Fi available.

€€ Iturrienea Ostatua, C Santa María, T944 161 500, www.iturrieneaostatua.com. This beautiful *pensión* in the heart of the Casco Viejo *pintxo* zone is carefully lined in stone, wood, art, and idiosyncratic objects. With delicious breakfasts (€4) and homely rooms, you might want to move in. Free Wi-Fi. Recommended.

€ Albergue Bilbao Aterpetxea, Ctra Basurto-Kastrexana 70, T944 270 054, http://albergue.bilbao.net. Bus No 58 from Plaza Circular and the bus station. Bilbao's HI hostel is a block-of-flats-sized structure by a motorway on the outskirts of Bilbao. Despite its inconvenient location, it does have good facilities (including bike hire). There's accommodation in dorms, singles or doubles; it's cheaper for under-25s, but *pensiones* in the centre are just as cheap. The 0930 check-out is a shock to the system when the rest of the nation runs with 1200.

€ Hostal Méndez, C Santa María 13, T944 160 364, www.pensionmendez.com. A dignified building with castle-sized doors and an entrance guarded by iron dogs. The 1st floor has *hostal*-grade rooms with new bathrooms, while the 4th floor is *pensión*-style accommodation, simpler, but still very adequate. Many rooms have balconies, but there's street noise until 2400 or later.

€ Pensión Ladero, C Lotería 1, T944 150 932, www.pensionladero.es. Right in the thick of it, this small and welcoming option has cork tiles, good shared bathrooms and very well-priced rooms with TV, some of which are reached by a tiny spiral staircase. There's some echoing noise but you'll receive a hearty Basque welcome – just as well, as it's on the 4th floor with no lift. Excellent value and the price doesn't change by season. Recommended. No bookings taken.

€ Pensión Manoli, C Libertad 2, T944 155 636, www.pensionmanoli.com. In the heart of the Casco Viejo with some good-value exterior rooms with balcony and shared bathroom. Bright and well looked after.

Bilbao's seafront *p36*
Staying here is a good alternative to the city; there are plenty of options.

€€€€ Hotel Embarcadero, Av Zugazarte 51, T944 803 100, www.hotelembarcadero. com; Metro Areeta. With an excellent seafront location, this grand old villa now houses an excellent boutique hotel. The spacious, attractive rooms come with modern flowery wallpaper; pay the little extra for a wide water view. Recommended.

€€€ Gran Hotel Puente Colgante, C María Díaz de Haro 2, T944 014 800, www. granhotelpuentecolgante.com. Euskotren

Portugalete; Metro Areeta. A reconstructed 19th-century building with a grand façade, this upmarket modern hotel is superbly situated next to the Puente Vizcaya on the waterfront promenade. All rooms face outwards, and the hotel has all the facilities you need. There are good discounted rates available via the website.

€€ Hotel Igeretxe, Playa de Ereaga s/n, T944 910 009, www.hoteligeretxe.com, Metro Neguri. Shaded by palms, this welcoming hotel is right on Ereaga beach, Getxo's main social strand. Formerly a *balneario*, the hotel still offers some spa facilities, as well as a restaurant overlooking the slightly grubby sand. Breakfast included.

€€ Pensión Usategi, C Landene 2, T944 913 918, Metro Bidezabal. Well placed on the headland above pretty Arrigunaga beach, the rooms are clean and cool, and some have great views.

€ Pensión Areeta, C Mayor 13 (Las Arenas), T944 638 136, Metro Areeta. Near the metro and an iron bar's throw from the Puente Vizcaya, this is a good place in the heart of the trendy Las Arenas district of Getxo. The rooms are smallish but welcoming.

Camping
Camping Sopelana, Ctra Bilbao-Plentzia s/n, T946 762 120, www.campingsopelana. com; Metro Sopelana. Very handy for the metro into Bilbao, this is the most convenient campsite within range of the city. Well equipped with facilities, and close to the shops, it's right by the beach, too. There are also 7 bungalows available.

🍴 Eating

Bilbao *p26, map p28*
Bilbao's Casco Viejo is undoubtedly the prime place to head for *pintxos* and evening drinking, with the best areas being the **Plaza Nueva** and around the **Siete Calles**, with a particularly earthy and vibrant Basque scene at the top of C Somera. There's another concentration of bars on **Av Licenciado Poza**

and the smaller **C García Rivero** off it. The narrow **C Ledesma**, a street back from Gran Vía, is a popular place to head for lunch set menus or after-work snacks and drinks. There are some good restaurants in the Casco Viejo (including a couple geared solely to tourists), but also plenty of options scattered through the New Town and Deustu.

ttt Arbola Gaña, Museo de Bellas Artes, Plaza del Museo s/n, T944 424 657. Decorated with modern minimalism, this restaurant upstairs in the fine arts museum makes a great spot for a lazy lunch while you admire the wonderful views. The food is elaborate, but with less flashiness than other upmarket spots around here. The quality of the ingredients is very high.

ttt Asador Ibáñez de Bilbao, C Ibáñez de Bilbao 6, T944 233 034, www.asadorIbanezdebilbao.com. This smart spot is a traditional meat restaurant specializing in roast lamb, which emerges from the kitchen in enormous chunks on traditional clay dishes and beautifully tender. Service is polite and there's also a good variety of fresh shellfish and crustaceans if the meat sounds a bit much.

ttt Guggenheim Restaurant, Av Abandoibarra 2, T944 239 333, www.restauranteguggenheim.com. A good all-round option in the museum. One of Spain's most highly regarded restaurants, this offers innovative gourmet cuisine in small but beautifully presented portions in its restaurant section. The degustation menu goes for €76 plus drinks – the wine list is excellent – but there's also a decent *menú del día* for €20 in the bistro section. The furniture is Gehry's work. No bookings are taken for the bistro, which is served (slowly) from 1330 on a 1st-come basis. Both the cafés do a fine line in croissants, coffee and *pintxos*; the one inside, off Gallery 104 has more seating and a nice view over the river.

ttt Guria, Gran Vía 66, T944 415 780, www.restauranteguria.com, Metro San Mamés. One of Bilbao's top restaurants with plush red walls and a quiet elegant atmosphere. Its stock-in-trade, like many of its

counterparts, is *bacalao*, which you'll never have better than here. Count on €60 a head minimum, more if you forsake the fish for the meat, which is tender and tasty: the steak tartare and the foie are both exquisite. A cheaper option is to eat in the bar, where there's a bistro menu. There's a very respectable selection of brandies too.

ttt Mina, Muelle Manzana s/n, T944 795 938, www.restaurantemina.es. Rated by many Bilbao foodies as the most enjoyable place to eat in town, this restaurant faces the Casco Viejo on the riverbank. Expect creative combinations that you haven't seen before and are unlikely to again. There's no menu, but the table d'hôte is excellent at €54 and beats more pretentious places that charge twice the price. Service is top notch. Recommended.

ttt Serantes and **Serantes II**, C Licenciado Poza 16 and Alameda Urquijo 51, T944 102 066 and 944 102 699, www.marisqueriaserantes.com, Metro Indautxu. These *marisquerías* (seafood restaurants) have a deservedly high reputation for the quality of their fish. It's all very fresh, and the chefs have the confidence to let the flavours of the seafood hold their own. Go with the daily special – it's usually excellent, or tackle some *cigalas* (Dublin Bay prawns) the 4WD of the prawn world, equipped with pincers. A third branch, **Serantes III**, is at Alameda Mazarredo 75, T944 248 004, opposite the Guggenheim.

ttt Víctor, Plaza Nueva 2, T944 151 678. A quality upstairs restaurant with an elegant but relaxed atmosphere. This is a top place to try Bilbao's signature dish, *bacalao al pil-pil*, or the restaurant's variation on it, and there's an excellent wine selection. Service is polite and formal. Don't confuse with **Víctor Montes**, also worthwhile and on the same square, see below. Recommended.

ttt Víctor Montes, Plaza Nueva 8, T944 155 603. This traditional and excellent restaurant is known for its huge collection of wines and whiskies. The elegant upstairs dining room has the best of Basque cuisine at surprisingly reasonable prices. Downstairs is a very popular *pintxo* bar; if you can shoulder your

Pintxos

In the Basque country, from about 1900 in the evening until midnight or so, everyone lives in the street, walking, talking, drinking and eating *pintxos*.

Wherever you go in the region, you'll be confronted and tempted by a massive array of food across the top of bars. Many bars serve up very traditional fare: slices of *tortilla* (potato omelette) or *pulgas de jamón* (small rolls with cured ham). Other bars, enthused by 'new Basque' cuisine, take things further and dedicate large parts of their day to creating miniature food sculptures using more esoteric ingredients. The key factor is that they're all meant to be eaten. Many places will prepare hot *pintxos* straight from the kitchen – these have to be ordered but are always well worth the wait. For the cold ones atop the bar, you can ask the bartender or usually simply help yourself to what you fancy, making sure to remember what you've had for the final reckoning. If you can't tell what something is, ask: *¿de qué es?*. *Pintxos* usually cost between €1.50 and €3 depending on the bar and ingredients.

way to it in the evening, you'll find that not a square inch is free of posh and delicious bites.

¶¶¶ Zortziko, Alameda Mazarredo 17, T944 239 743, www.zortziko.es. This upmarket business-district choice focuses on fairly traditional Basque ingredients brought to perfection with modern techniques. Squid with liquid foie gras or slow-cooked pigeon breast are signature dishes, but the €92 degustation menu is the best way to see the full range of this Michelin-starred restaurant's repertoire.

¶¶ Asian Chic, C Ledesma 30, T944 231 186. Right in the heart of the Bilbao business district, this elegant and extensive Japanese/Chinese restaurant is a favourite lunch escape for its speedily served *menú del día*, which might include tasty sushi followed by glazed duck breast and fried rice. There are also good sashimi and tempura options à la carte, and teppanayaki for group bookings.

¶¶ Casa Vasca, Av Lehendakari Aguirre 13-15, T944 483 980, www.casavasca.com. A Deustu institution on the main road – the front bar has a good selection of posh *pintxos* and a couple of comfortable nooks to settle down with a slightly pricey drink. Behind is a restaurant that serves pretty authentic Basque cuisine in generous portions. Another dining room serves a cheap *menú del día*, and there's even a nightclub downstairs, catering for an older crowd.

¶¶ Colmado Ibérico, Alameda Urquijo 20, T944 436 001. A feast of piggy products, this welcoming locale is both a ham shop and a bar/restaurant, where you can munch on a basic (but delicious) *pulga* of Spain's finest ham or more elaborate pork-based creations.

¶¶ Egiluz, C Perro 4, T944 150 242. Among all the bright modern lights of the Casco Viejo's newer restaurants, this sturdy old family-run place is still the place to go if you fancy a steak or similar. The dining room is upstairs at the back of the bar. They serve a huge *chuletón* – it could comfortably feed 2 – and other excellent grilled and roasted fare.

¶¶ Hostaria Marchese del Porto, C Marqués del Puerto 10, T944 161 680, Metro Moyúa. This elegant Italian restaurant goes slightly over the top with its decor but is deservedly popular with local businessfolk at lunchtime. Good pasta and gelati too.

¶¶ Kasko, C Santa María 16, T944 160 311, www.restaurantekasko.com. With funky, appealing decor inspired by the fish and high-class but low-priced new Basque food, this spacious bar-restaurant is always busy, and is in the heart of the action. Service is bohemian-friendly, and there's sometimes a pianist accompanying your meal. The daily *menú del día* is good value, and there are always interesting specials on the evening menu.

¶¶ La Viña, C Henao 27, T944 243 602; Metro Moyúa. You could easily miss this tiny bar wedged into a block in the Ensanche. As well as being a hospitable place to have a glass of wine, they serve some very fine food at a very fair price. Their speciality is seafood, with mussels, crabs, or whatever's fresh to choose from and eat at the handful of small tables.

¶¶ Su@, C Marqués del Puerto 4, T944 232 292, www.sua.es. Metro Moyúa. One of the best of the recent designer restaurants to open in Bilbao, this is ultra-modern but comfortable, with a romantic coloured lighting scheme and a menu of new-style creations that are curiously ordered by temperature that they leave the kitchen at. A gimmick, yes, but the food and atmosphere are pretty good. There's a *menú del día* for €17.50. Evening bookings essential.

¶¶ Taloaska, Av Madariaga 7, T944 758 264, www.taloaska.com. A more than solid choice in the heart of Deustu, with a bar that stretches as far as the eye can see and is very well endowed with *pintxos*. At the end is the dining room, where there's a good *menú* for €11.

¶ Capuccino, C Gordóniz 2, T944 436 980. A place for people in the know. This café, run by a friendly Egyptian, and with a map of the old Nile painted on the roof, serves filled pitta rolls, as well as *shawarma*, *musaka*, and other snacks. They have an excellent range of teas.

¶ Garibolo, C Fernández del Campo 7, T944 223 255, Metro Moyúa. Opens for lunch Mon-Sat, and dinner Fri-Sat. There are now a few vegetarian restaurants in Bilbao, but this, the original, is still the best. The colourful Garibolo packs 'em in, particularly for its €12.50 lunch special. No alcohol served.

¶ Laga, C Merced 2, T944 164 770. This bright, simply decorated bar is one of the Casco's best places for simple, no-nonsense wholesome Basque food. Particularly recommended are the croquettes, but it's all good, including the fresh fish, the garlicky steaks and the *mollejas*. Great value.

¶ Mr Lee, C Pedro Martínez Artola 12, T944 440 862. Free of the repetitive paraphernalia that adorns other Chinese restaurants in Spain, which tend to become caricatures of themselves, this has an elegant, spacious dining area with Asian artwork of restrained good taste. The menu has a range of decent dishes from different parts of east and southeast Asia. Good value. The street slopes up from Plaza Zabálburu.

¶ New Inn, Alameda Urquijo 9, T944 151 043. The restored art nouveau splendour of the main bar of this popular lunch-spot is reason enough to enter. Workers in Bilbao offices sadly have little time now to grab a 3-course meal, so this place caters for them with a range of excellent sandwiches and similar.

¶ Río Oja, C Perro 4, T944 150 871. Another good option on this street, specializing in bubbling Riojan stews and Basque fish dishes, most of which are in big casseroles at the bar. The dishes will come microwave-heated (standard practice in Spain), but it's good value and has friendly service.

¶ Rotterdam, C Perro 6, T944 162 165. Small, uncomplicated Casco Viejo restaurant with a *simpático* boss. This is what lunch restaurants have always been like here, with a solid *menú del día* for €9.

¶ Saibigain, C Barrenkale Barrena 16, T944 150 123. Closed Sun. This is an intensely traditional and atmospheric place, and one of the best cheap restaurants in the Casco Viejo. It's full of black and white photos of Athletic Bilbao, and has a phalanx of hams hanging over the bar. There's a *menú del día* for €9, and various other set meals from about €20 per person; it's worth waiting to grab a table upstairs.

Pintxo bars

¶¶ Bar Irrintzi, C Santa María 8, T944 167 616, www.irrintzi.es. With a vibe so laid-back that there's not even a till: the takings are under colour-coordinated bottles behind the bar, this Casco Viejo bar doesn't skimp on the quality. *Pintxos* are an art form, with a superb array of imaginative snacks, all carefully labelled, freshly made and delicious.

¶¶ Berton, C Jardines 11, T944 167 035. The hanging *jamones* and bunches of grapes define this cheerful bar, which has top-notch ham *pintxos* and *raciones* and some quality wines by the glass. It's mushroomed in recent years, and now has another bar around the corner and one opposite. All offer better value for tapas at the bar than sit-down meals.

¶¶ Café-Bar Bilbao, Plaza Nueva 6, T944 151 671. A sparky place with top service and a selection of some of the better gourmet *pintxos* (all labelled) to be had around the old town. It's always busy, but the bar staff never seem to miss a trick.

¶¶ Gatz, C Santa María 10, T944 154 861. A convivial bar with warm, non-designer decor and some of the Casco's better *pintxos*, which are frequent contenders in the awards for such things. Happily spills on to the street at weekends. Friendly, no-nonsense staff. Recommended.

¶¶ El Globo, C Diputación 8, T944 154 221. There's an extraordinary variety of cold and cooked-to-order hot *pintxos* at this place near the Moyúa square. Traditional bites take their place alongside wildly imaginative modern creations. Recommended.

¶¶ Lekeitio, C Diputación 1, T944 239 240. An attentive bar that's a mile long with a fantastic selection of simple after-work eats. The variety of fishy and seafoody *pintxos* are good, as is the *tortilla*. A palisade of oars and life-buoys sections off a small sit-down eating area.

¶¶ Okela, C García Rivero 8, T944 415 937. A modern bar popular with the office crowd and dominated by a huge signed photo of the footballer Joseba Etxebarría in full stride for Athletic Bilbao. Decent *pintxos*. There are several other good choices on this street.

¶¶ Oriotarra, C Blas de Otero 30, T944 470 830. A classy *pintxo* bar in Deustu that has won an award for the best bar-top snack in Bilbao. A round of applause for the pig's ear *millefeuille*.

¶¶ Urkia, C Somera 40, T606 990 295. One of the more popular bars at the top of Somera, which buzzes with a pro-Basque after-work crowd from all social strata, this has elaborate *pintxos* presented on slate tablets. They change regularly, but at last visit the anchovy, brie, caviar, and tempura courgette combination was mighty impressive.

¶¶ Xukela, C Perro 2, T944 159 772. A very social bar on a very social street. Attractive *pintxos* and some good sit-down food – cheeses and cured meats – and a clientele upending glasses of Rioja at competitive pace until comparatively late.

¶ Artajo, C Ledesma 7, T944 248 596, Metro Abando. Uncomplicated and candid bar, one of many on this street, with homely wooden tables and chairs and good traditional snacks of tortilla and *pulgas de jamón*. Famous for its *tigres* (mussels in spicy tomato sauce).

¶ Jaunak, C Somera 10, T944 159 979. One of quite a few earthy, friendly Basque bars on this street, with a huge range of large *bocadillos* at about €3.50 a shot.

¶ Kuku Soak, C Barrenkale Barrena 18, T944 163 807. On a busy Casco Viejo corner, this bar doesn't mind turning the music up pretty loud, but that doesn't bother the cheerful mix of after-workers and students. Its main temptation is its wide range of *pulgas* (little sandwichy *pintxos*) with various gourmet combinations of fillings: mark your choices on the tear-off sheets, and they'll be freshly made. You can also order to take away.

¶ Taberna Taurina, C Ledesma 5. A tiny old-time tiles 'n' sawdust bar, which is packed top to bottom with bullfighting memorabilia. It's fascinating to browse the old pictures, which convey something of the controversial activity's noble side. The *tortilla* here also commands respect.

Cafés

Boulevard, C Arenal 3, T946 791 752. This fabulous historic café was once Bilbao's literary meeting place. Now 140 years old, it still has plenty of atmosphere as theatre-goers, workers, students and tourists coincide in its cavernous interior. There's a very glamorous downstairs cocktail bar, but the art deco upstairs is what the place is all about.

Café Iruña, Jardines de Albia s/n, T944 237 021. This noble old establishment on the Jardines de Albia has begun its 2nd century in style and is more popular than ever, with people spilling out onto the street. Well refurbished, the large building is divided into a smarter café/restaurant space with wood panelling in neo-Moorish style, and a tiled bar with old sherry ads and some good *pintxos* – including lamb kebabs sizzling on the grill in the corner.

Café La Granja, Plaza Circular 3, T944 230 813. A spacious old Bilbao café, opened in 1926. Its high ceilings and long bar are designed to cope with the lively throng that gathers throughout the day. Attractive art nouveau fittings and *pintxos*, although the simple *menú del día* is a little overpriced.

Café Lamiak, C Pelota 8, T944 161 765. A peaceful and likeable 2-floor forum, the sort of place a literary genre, pressure group or world-famous band might start out. It's a mixed gay/straight crowd, with a relaxed atmosphere.

El Kiosko del Arenal, Muelle del Arenal s/n, T657 711 352. Elegant and cool café under the bandstand in the Arenal. Plenty of outdoor tables overlooking the river. Barbecue in the corner. Recommended.

Bilbao's seafront *p36*

There's plenty of good eating in these waterside suburbs.

¶¶¶ **Asador El Puerto/Zabala**, C Aretxondo 20, T944 912 166, Metro Algorta. With fresh seafood right off the boats and a great location by Getxo's old port, this makes a prime fish-eating destination. There's no menu: they just tell you what's fresh that day. Prices can add up, but the quality shines through.

¶¶¶ **Cubita**, Ctra Galea 30, T944 911 700, www.cubita.biz, Metro Neguri. A highly acclaimed restaurant with a new location by the windmill above Arrigunaga beach. People rave about the *cigalas* (Dublin bay prawns) turned out by young modern chef Alvaro Martínez.

¶¶¶ **Jolastoky**, Av Leioa 24, T944 912 031, www.restaurantejolastoki.com, Metro Neguri. Decorated in classy but homely country-mansion style, Jolastoky is a house of good repute throughout Euskadi. Definitely traditional in character, dishes such as *caracoles en salsa vizcaína* (snails) and *liebre* (hare) are the sort of treats that give Basque cuisine its lofty reputation.

¶¶ **Karola Etxea**, C Aretxondo 22, T944 600 868, Metro Algorta. Perfectly situated in a quiet lane above the old port. It's a good, not too expensive place to try some fish; there are usually a few available, such as *txitxarro* (scad) or *besugo* (sea bream). The *kokotxas* (cheeks and throats of hake in sauce) are also delicious.

¶ **El Hule**, C Victor Chavarri 13, T944 722 104. In the narrow, sloping streets of Portugalete's old town (just behind the town hall on the waterfront near the Puente Colgante), this is a cracking spot for lunch. The small but cute upstairs and downstairs dining rooms are cosy and comfortable. The food is traditional, uncomplicated fare (*menú del día* €12) served with a smile and plenty of quality.

¶ **Irrintzi**, C Particular de Arlamendi, off C Zalama, T944 643 372. This homely bar has appealing brick and wood decor, an upmarket clientele and about the finest reputation for *pintxos* on the right bank of the ría. There's an excellent array, and they are all very tempting. From Metro Areeta, head straight ahead and up the hill past the Mandarin Chinese restaurant, and turn right. The bar is un-signed.

◑ Bars and clubs

Bilbao *p26, map p28*

Bilbao's nightlife is very quiet during the week, but it makes up for it at weekends. Most bars have to shut at 0400 these days, but there are some *discotecas* that go later. Nearly everywhere in the Casco Viejo shuts by 0130, but you can always dash across the Puente de la Merced to the streets around C Hernani, where there is plenty going on. Be careful in this zone though, as muggings are not unknown. There are lots of bars in the Casco Viejo, including many on the legendary streets of Ronda, Somera and Barenkale, the latter legendary for its boisterous rock 'n' roll scene.

Bars
Bizitza, C Torre 1, T944 165 882. Very chilled mixed gay-straight bar with a Basque political slant. Relaxed, atmospheric and welcoming, with frequent cultural events. One of the top spots for an after-dinner *copa* in Bilbao – they mix a great drink. Recommended.
Compañía del Ron, C Máximo Aguirre 23, T944 213 069. Friends of Ronald will be happy here, with over 100 rums at the disposal of the bar staff, who know how to handle them. Despite the chain-pub feel (it's not), this is a good early-evening spot in the heart of the new town.
El Patio de mi Casa, C Cosme Echevarrieta 13, T944 248 676. A small but quality place, which serves great *copa*s to a discerning crowd in a homely, relaxed atmosphere. Open nightly 2300-0300.
Errondabide, C Ronda 20. This is a good place to come to get a feel of what a hardline pro-independence Basque bar is like. There are political posters everywhere, photos of ETA prisoners, a spirited atmosphere, and plenty of smoke and beer.
Luz Gas, C Pelota 6, T944 790 823. A beautiful mood bar with an oriental touch. Sophisticated but friendly, and you can challenge all-comers to chess or Connect-4.
Muga, C María Muñoz 8, T944 162 781. A long-time favourite, this relaxed café and bar has a rock 'n' roll vibe, with colourful tables, fanzines and CDs for sale, and a down-to-earth clientele.
Zodiako's, C Euskal Herria s/n (corner of Telletxe), T944 604 059, Metro Algorta. This squiggly bar in the heart of Getxo is one of the best, with a terrace, *pintxos* and service with a smile. There's a *discoteca* underneath.

Zulo, Barrenkale 22. A tiny nationalist bar with plenty of plastic fruit and a welcoming set. The impressively bearded owner Txema is a notable Casco Viejo character.

Clubs
Bullitt Groove Club, C Dos de Mayo 3, T944 165 291, www.myspace.com/bullittgrooveclub. Across the river from the Casco Viejo, this retro discobar has a variety of music styles. On Sat, it's Black Roots night, with excellent soul and R&B. Other nights offer ska, reggae and 1960s rock.
Conjunto Vacío, C Muelle de la Merced 3, T944 158 338, www.conjuntovacio.net. Empty by name and packed by nature, at least from about 2 on Fri and Sat nights. The music is fairly light *bakalao*, the crowd mixed and good-looking, the drinks horrendously expensive, but entry is usually free.
El Balcón de La Lola, C Bailén 10, www.balcondelalola.com. Decorated in industrial style with sheet-metal and graffiti, this is a weekend-opening club that varies in character from fairly cheesy dance to pretty heavy garage. Open latish; concerts earlier in the night.
Santana 27, C Tellería 27, Bolueta, T944 598 617, www.santana27.com. Open nightly 2300-0600. Near the metro station in Bolueta, this vast venue has opened out here to avoid the strict opening hours in central Bilbao. There are so many dance floors that you are bound to find something you like; it often has live bands and special club nights. Usually €5-10 to get in, including a drink.

Entertainment

Bilbao *p26, map p28*
For bullfighting and football, see page 35.

Cinema
Cines Renoir, C Lehendakari Aguirre 23, T944 751 210, www.cinesrenoir.com, Metro Deustu. This is one of the better central cinemas.

Music venues

Bilbo Rock, Muelle de la Merced s/n, T944 151 306. Atmospheric venue in a converted church that is now a temple of live rock with bands playing most nights of the week. No licence, but canned beer from machines.

Kafe Antzokia, C San Vicente 2, T944 244 625, www.kafeantzokia.com. An ex-cinema turned Bilbao icon, this is a live venue for anything from death metal to Euskara poetry, and features 2 spacious floors with bars which go late and loud at weekends. Sociable, friendly, and a place where you might hear more Euskara than Spanish.

Palacio Euskalduna, C Abandoibarra 4, T944 310 310, www.euskalduna.net. Top-quality classical performances from the symphonic orchestras of Bilbao and Euskadi, as well as high-profile Spanish and international artists.

Theatre

Teatro Arriaga, Plaza Arriaga 1, T944 792 036, www.teatroarriaga.com. Bilbao's highest-profile theatre is picturesquely set on the river by the Casco Viejo. It's a plush treat of a place in late 19th-century style, but the work it presents can be very innovative. The better seats go for €25 and above, but there are often decent pews available for just €5.

⊛ **Festivals and events**

Bilbao *p26, map p28*
Sat after 15 Aug Aste Nagusia (big week), Bilbao's major fiesta, follows on from those in Vitoria and San Sebastián to make a month of riotous Basque partying. It is a boisterous mixture of everything: concerts, *corridas*, traditional Basque sports and serious drinking.

O Shopping

Bilbao *p26, map p28*
Bilbao is the best place to shop in Northern Spain. The majority of mainstream Spanish and international clothing stores are in the Ensanche, particularly on and around C Ercilla.

The Casco Viejo harbours dozens of quirkier shops. A new commercial centre, **Zubiarte**, just by the Puente de Deustu, has a full complement of fashion chains and a cinema. **Mercado de la Ribera**, the art deco market by the river where stallholders used to come for the weekly market, has over 400 stalls selling fruit, veg, meat and fish, it's the major centre for fresh produce in Bilbao. Come in the morning if you want to get the true flavour; afternoons are comparatively quiet.

There are numerous great delis for buying Basque and Spanish produce; **Txorierri**, in the old town at Artekale 19, is one, **Oka**, at Marqués del Puerto 1 near Plaza Moyúa, is another.

▲ Activities and tours

Bilbao *p26, map p28*
A double-decker tour bus (www.bus turistikoa.com) runs around the city, stopping 15 times in the standard hop-on, hop-off circuit. A 24-hr ticket is €12.
Bilbao Paso a Paso, T944 730 078, www.bilbaopasoapaso.com. Knowledgeable tours of Bilbao and the whole of Euskadi that can be tailored to suit.
Bilboats, T644 442 055, www.bilboats.com. Boat trips along the Nervión. The basic €10 jaunt takes you up past the Guggenheim – have the cameras ready – but the longer €16 trip takes you right up to the sea, past the ghosts of the city's industrial past.

Bilbao's seafront *p36*
Getxo Abentura, www.getxo.net. The Getxo tourist office can organize just about any outdoor activity you can think of in the Getxo area, from caving to canoeing, provided there are enough people to make a go of it (usually 4 for group-style outings).
Náutica Getxo, Puerto Deportivo de Getxo, T609 985 977, www.nauticagetxo.com. On the jetty at the end of Ereaga beach, this company hires out yachts with or without a skipper. Sailing knowledge isn't required as the boats come with auxiliary power, but if you want to learn, these guys can teach you that too.

Bilbao p26, map p28

Air

Bilbao's airport near **Sondika/Loiu**, 10 km northeast of the centre, is a beautiful building designed by Santiago Calatrava, seemingly in homage to the whale. A taxi to/from town costs about €20-25. There's an efficient bus service that runs to/from Bilbao's bus station via Plaza Moyúa in central Bilbao. It leaves from outside the terminal, takes 20-30 mins and runs every half hour. One-way €1.30.

Bilbao is served from several European destinations. The cheapest direct flights from the **UK** are with the budget operators **EasyJet** and **Vueling**. Bilbao is also directly connected with several other European cities. Note that although **Ryanair** seem to fly to Bilbao, the flights actually land at Santander, from where a bus service runs to Bilbao. Bilbao also has frequent domestic connections with **Madrid**, **Barcelona** and other Spanish cities, operated by **Iberia** and **Spanair**.

Airlines offices Iberia, C Ercilla 20, Bilbao, T944 245 506, www.iberia.es; Spanair, Aeropuerto de Bilbao, T944 869 498, www.spanair.com.

Bicycle hire

Alquimoto, C Anselma de Salces 9, T944 012 563, www.alquimoto.com, rent bikes, scooters and motorbikes.

Boat

The Portsmouth–Bilbao ferry is now a thing of the past. The Basque government were making noises about subsidising a replacement service, but it at time of writing it seemed unlikely to happen. The closest ferry connection from the UK is to Santander.

Bus

The majority of Bilbao's inter-urban buses leave from the Termibus station near the football stadium (Metro San Mamés, tram stops outside). All long-haul destinations are served from here, but several Basque towns are served from the stops next to Abando station on C Hurtado Amezaga.

To **San Sebastián**: buses from the Termibus station every 30 mins weekdays, every hour at weekends, operated by PESA (1 hr 20 mins, €10). To **Vitoria**: buses from the Termibus station about every 30 mins with **Autobuses La Un ón** (55 mins, €6). Other destinations include **Santander** (almost hourly, 1 hr 30 mins, from €7), **Pamplona** (7-9 daily, €2 hrs), **Logroño** (5 daily, 2 hrs), and **Burgos** (4 direct daily, 2 hrs).

Car

Though the centre is fairly well signposted, the 1-way system and extensive pedestrianization can make it difficult to find your way around. Parking in the centre is metered; if your hotel doesn't have private parking, you're best off in one of the underground stations, which cost around €15-18 for 24 hrs. The handiest for the Casco Viejo is **Arenal**; cross the Puente del Ayuntamiento from the new town and turn right. When approaching Bilbao by road from the east, it's worth paying the €1.75 (max) toll through the Artxanda tunnel, which brings you in to town right alongside the Guggenheim Museum, saving much time and potential to get lost.

Car hire The usual assortment of multinationals dominate. The process is fairly painless, and national driving licences are accepted. **Atesa**, C Sabino Arana 9, T944 423 290; Aeropuerto de Bilbao, T944 533 340, www.atesa.es; **Avis**, Av Doctor Areilza 34, T944 275 760; Aeropuerto de Bilbao, T944 869 648, www.avis.com; **Hertz**, C Doctor Achucarro 10, T944 153 677; Aeropuerto de Bilbao, T944 530 931, www.hertz.com.

Metro

Bilbao's metro (www.metrobilbao.net) runs Sun-Thu until about 2400, Fri until about 0200, and 24 hrs on Sat. A single fare costs from €1.40, while a day pass is €4. There's 1 main line running through the city and out to the beach suburbs, while the second line heads out to the coast on the other side of the estuary.

Tram

A single costs €1.25; there are machines at the tram stops. It runs every 10-15 mins or so. You have to validate your ticket in the machine on the platform before boarding.

Train

Bilbao has 3 train stations. The main one, **Abando**, is the terminal of **RENFE**, the national Spanish railway. It's far from a busy network but it's the principal mainline service.

Abando is also the main terminus for **Euskotren**, a handy short-haul train network that connects Bilbao and San Sebastián with many of the smaller Basque towns as well as their own outlying suburbs. The other Bilbao base for these trains is **Atxuri**, situated just east of the Casco Viejo, an attractive but run-down station for lines running eastwards as far as San Sebastián. These are particularly useful for reaching the towns of Euskadi's coast. **Gernika** is serviced every hour and on to **Mundaka** and **Bermeo**. Trains to **San Sebastián** run every hour on the hour (2 hrs 40 mins) via **Zarautz**, **Zumaia**, **Eibar**, and **Durango**.

Narrow-gauge FEVE trains connect Bilbao along the coast to **Santander**, 3 times daily (2½ hrs) and beyond. They are slow but scenic and leave from the Estación de Santander just next to Bilbao's main Abando railway station. There's also a daily service from here to **León** (7 hrs 15 mins).

Getxo *p36*
Bus
Buses No 3411 and No 3413 run to/from Plaza Moyúa every 30 mins.

Metro
Getxo is a large area, and the metro stations Areeta, Gobela, Neguri, Aiboa, Algorta, and Bidezabal all fall within its area. The beaches further on can be accessed from Larrabasterra, Sopelana and Plentzia metros.

Portugalete *p37*
Bus
Bus No 3152 from the Arenal bus station in Bilbao (Mon-Sat).

Metro
Bilbao's Metro (Line 2) now runs to Portugalete; the Line 1 station of Areeta is also handy, just across the Puente Colgante.

Train
From Abando station, the **Euskotren** service runs to Portugalete (line: Santurtzi) every 12 mins weekdays, less frequently at weekends, and takes 20 mins.

🛈 Directory

Bilbao *p26, map p28*
Consulates Eire, T944 912 575; France, T944 249 000; Germany, T944 238 585; South Africa, T944 641 124; UK, T944 157 600; USA, the nearest consular representative is at the embassy in Madrid, T915 872 200. **Internet** There are various free Wi-Fi zones around the centre of Bilbao, including Plaza Nueva. El Señor de la Red, Alameda de Rekalde 14, T944 237 425, €2/hr; Laser Internet, C Sendeja 5, T944 453 509, Mon-Fri 1030-0230, Sat and Sun 1100-0230, €0.05 per min, handy and quick, also offers photocopier and fax services; Ciber Latino, C Carnicería Vieja 6, internet at €2 per hr; La Basca Universal, C Viuda de Epalza 12, T944 792 865, cheap phone calls and internet on the Arenal. **Language schools** Instituto Hemingway, C Bailén 5, T944 167 901, www.institutohemingway.com. **Laundry** Fast & Clean, Plaza Ensanche 9, T944 239 363. Dry cleaning and service washes. **Medical services** Hospital de Basurto, Av Montevideo 18, T944 006 000, T944 755 000, Tram Basurto. **Police** The emergency number for all necessities is T112, while T092 will take you to the local police. **Main police station**, Policía Municipal Bilbao, C Luis Briñas 14, T944 205 000. **Post office** Main post office, Alameda Urquijo 19; Casco Viejo branch, C Epalza 4 (opposite Arenal).

San Sebastián/Donostia

The sweep of La Concha bay and the hills overlooking it draw comparisons for San Sebastián with Rio de Janeiro. One of the peninsula's most beautiful cities, it's a place with a light and leisurely feel, and draws throngs of summer holidaymakers. With a superb natural setting, lovely sandy beaches, and a regular influx of international stardom during its film festival, it's a relaxed and enjoyable place that has been invigorated by the addition of two excellent museums and a piece of world-class modern architecture in the Kursaal auditorium. It's also the gourmet capital of Spain, whether you splash out on sumptuous degustation menus in gastronomic temples or graze elaborate pintxos in the livewire bars.

   The pedestrianized Old Town lies at the foot of the Monte Urgull hill, and is unabashedly devoted to tapas bars; the pintxos here are astoundingly inventive, small works of art in their own right. The bars are in constant competition to take gourmet cuisine in miniature one step further. From the old town, the main beach stretches west right around the bay to steep Monte Igueldo, the spot to head for if you want your holiday snaps to have that panoramic postcard feel. The hills behind town are green and studded with villages that seem totally oblivious to the city's presence. This is where cider is made: in spring when the stuff's ready, people descend like locusts on the cider houses to drink it straight from the vat and eat enormous meals over sawdust floors. It's amazing any cider's left to be bottled. ⏵ *For listings, see pages 59-67.*

Ins and outs

Getting there San Sebastián's airport is at Hondarribia, 20 km east of the city (see page 68). It's connected with Madrid and Barcelona. Most inter-urban buses leave from the main bus station on Plaza Pío XII. Regular buses leave to and from Plaza Guipúzcoa to the outlying districts. San Sebastián's main **RENFE** terminus is the Estación del Norte just across the river from the new town area. ▸▸ *See Transport, page 66.*

Getting around San Sebastián is reasonably compact and most sights are within easy walking distance of each other. Buses run from one end of the city to the other.

Tourist information The efficient, English-speaking San Sebastián **tourist office** ① *Boulevard 8, T943 481 166, www.sansebastianturismo.com, Mon-Thu 0900-1330, 1530-1900 (1630-2000 in summer), Fri-Sat 0930-1900 (2000 in summer), Sun 1000-1400,* is busy but helpful. You can download city information to your mobile phone here. There's also a summer information kiosk on the beach promenade. The tourist office runs a booking agency for accommodation and events, www.sansebastianreservas.com, T902 443 442.

Background

San Sebastián is well past its days as a significant port or military bastion though it still has a small fishing fleet. Ever since royalty began summering here in the 19th century, the city has settled into its role of elegant seaside resort to the manner born. It was once, however, one of the important ports of Northern Spain, part of the *Hermandad de las Marismas* trading alliance from the 13th century on. In the 18th century, the Basques established a monopoly over the chocolate trade with Venezuela centred on this city. San Sebastián suffered during the Peninsular War: captured by the French, it was then besieged by English, Spanish and Portuguese forces. The valiant French garrison held out on the Monte Urgull hill for another week after the town had fallen, while the victorious British, Spanish and Portuguese pillaged the town. They also managed to set it on fire; Calle 31 de Agosto was the only street to survive the blaze. This was just one of several 'Great Fires' the city has endured.

Parte Vieja (Old Town)

The liveliest part of San Sebastián is its old section at the eastern end of the bay. Although most of it was destroyed by the 1813 fire, it is still full of character, with a dense concentration of *pintxo* bars, *pensiones*, restaurants and shops. Protecting the narrow streets is the solid bulk of **Monte Urgull**, which also shelters the small harbour area.

El Muelle

One of the city's nicest meanders is along Paseo Nuevo, which runs around the hill from the river mouth to the harbour. Beyond the town hall, San Sebastián's small fishing and recreational harbour, El Muelle, is a pleasant place to stroll around. There's a handful of cafés and tourist shops, and you can see the fishermen working on their boats while their wives mend the nets by the water. Halfway round the harbour is a monument to 'Aita Mari' (father Mari), the nickname of a local boatman who became a hero for his fearless acts of rescue of other sailors in fierce storms off the coast. In 1866 he perished in view of thousands attempting yet another rescue in a terrible tempest.

San Sebastián/Donostia

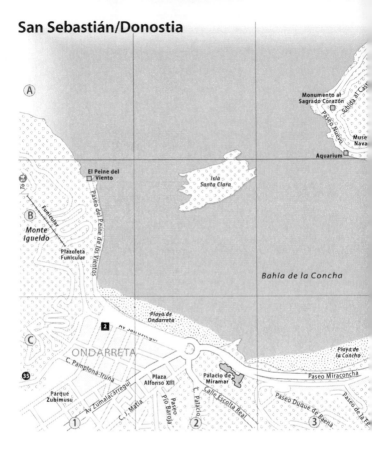

San Sebastián detail

N

200 metres
200 yards

Sleeping
De Londres y
  de Inglaterra **3** *B4*
Ezeiza **2** *C1*
Hostal Alemana **1** *C4*
Izar Bat **7** *detail*
María Cristina **12** *B5*

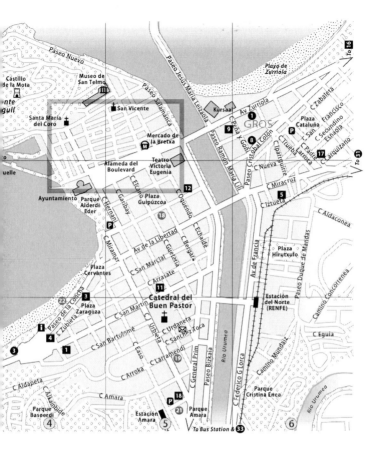

The **Museo Naval** ⓘ *Paseo del Muelle 24, T943 430 051, Tue-Sat 1000-1330, 1600-1930, Sun 1100-1400, €1.20*, is a harbourside museum, which unfortunately makes a potentially intriguing subject slightly dry and lifeless. While there's plenty of information about Basque seafaring, the interesting aspects are hurried over and there's little attempt to engage the visitor. Descriptions are in Spanish and Euskara only.

At the end of the harbour, San Sebastián's **aquarium** ⓘ *Plaza Carlos Blasco de Imaz s/n, T943 440 099, www.aquariumss.com, Tue-Thu 1000-1900 (2100 in summer), Fri-Sun 1000-2000 (2200 in summer), €12 (€6 for kids)*, is well stocked. The highlight is a tank brimming with fish, turtles, rays and a couple of portly sharks to keep the rest of them honest. There's a perspex tunnel through the tank, which can be viewed from above. Unfortunately, there's not much in the way of identification panels and viewing space can get crowded, particularly around shark-feeding time (Tuesday-Sunday at 1200), which isn't quite as dramatic as it sounds. Most fascinating are the shark egg cases, in which you can observe the tiny embryos. There is a bar/restaurant and shop on site.

Monte Urgull

The bulk of Monte Urgull is one of several Donostia spots that you can climb up to appreciate the view. An important defensive position until the city walls were taken down in 1863, it saw action from the 12th century onwards in several battles. The hill is topped by a small fort, the **Castillo de la Mota** ⓘ *daily 1100-1330, 1700-2000, summer only*, once used as the residence of the town's *alcalde* and as a prison. It has a small collection of old weapons, including a sword that belonged to the last Moorish king Boabdil. There's also a large statue of Christ, the **Monumento al Sagrado Corazón**, adding to San Sebastián's credentials as a Rio lookalike.

Motorboats to Isla Santa Clara in the middle of the bay leave from Monte Urgull, as do boats offering cruises round the harbour.

Iglesia de Santa María del Coro

In the heart of the old town, and with a façade about as ornate as Spanish baroque ever got, the church of Santa María del Coro squats under the rocks of Monte Urgull and faces the newer cathedral across the city. After the exuberant exterior, the interior is a contrast of low lighting, heavy oil paintings and incense. Above the altar is a large depiction of the man the city was named after, unkindly known by some as the 'pincushion saint' for the painful way he was martyred. Facing him at the other end of the nave is a stone crucifix in the unmistakable style of Eduardo Chillida, the late Basque sculptor (see box, above).

Museo de San Telmo

ⓘ *Plaza Zuloaga 1, T943 424 970, www.museosantelmo.com, Tue-Fri 1000-1400, 1500-1730, Sat-Sun 1000-1730, free. Currently closed for renovation.*
The San Telmo museum, set in a 16th-century Dominican convent, is worth a visit if only for its perfect Renaissance cloister set around a green lawn. The ground floor of the museum has a dedicated space for temporary exhibitions and a series of grave markers paired with evocative poetic quotes on death. Upstairs is mostly devoted to painting and sculpture. Fittingly, as the museum sits on a square named after him, Ignacio Zuloaga is well represented. A worthy successor to the likes of Velázquez and Goya in the art of portrait painting, one of the best examples here is his Columbus, who is deep and soulful (and suspiciously Basque-looking). There's also a small memorial to Zuloaga in the plaza outside. Upstairs, the gallery of Basque painting is a good place to get an idea of how

Bitter and twisted

You can't go far in the Basque lands without coming across a hauntingly contorted figure or sweep of rusted iron that signals a creation of Jorge de Oteiza or Eduardo Chillida. The powerful and original work of these two Basque sculptors is emblematic of the region.

Jorge de Oteiza, forthright and uncompromising well into his 90s, was born in Orio in 1908. After ditching a medical career in favour of sculpture he taught in South America. His big breakthrough came when commissioned to create pieces for the façade of the visionary new monastery at Arantzazu in the early 1950s. With his grey beard, leather jacket, beret and thick glasses, Oteiza cut quite a figure on site, but the anguish and power he managed to channel into his Apostles and Pietá was quite extraordinary. The Vatican prevented the erection of the 14 apostles for two decades. Oteiza was always preoccupied with relevance, famously saying that "a monument will be no more than a pile of stones or a coil of wire if it does not contribute to the making of a better human being, if it is not … the moulded key to a new kind of man".

Eduardo Chillida was born in 1924 in San Sebastián and in his youth (and before a knee injury) appeared between the sticks for Real Sociedad. A sculptor of huge world renown, the spaces he created within his work are as important as the materials that comprise it. The Peine de los Vientos at San Sebastián and the Plaza de los Fueros in Vitoria are designed to interact dynamically with their setting, while his exploration of oxidized iron as a medium was particularly appropriate for Euskadi, built on the glories of a now-faded iron industry. Softer work in alabaster and wood is less confronting, but evokes the same theme of space. Chillida-Leku museum outside San Sebastián houses a large cross-section of his massive output.

The two sculptors were on bitter terms for many years: Oteiza, perhaps jealous of Chillida's rising profile, held the view that he had 'sold out', refused to use his name, and criticized him bitterly in public. Over the years there were accusations of plagiarism from both sides. Oteiza eventually had a change of heart and after many peaceful overtures were rejected, they finally buried the hatchet in 1997 with the 'Zabalaga embrace'. In fact, it seems that before Chillida's death in August 2002, aged 78, they had become firm friends. Oteiza died only months later, in April 2003, aged 94.

different the local landscapes and physiques are to those of Spain; the quality is good, although there's not a sniff of the controversial, political or avant-garde.

Iglesia de San Vicente
The most interesting of San Sebastián's churches, San Vicente is a castle-like sandstone building that squats in the northeast of Parte Vieja. Started in the early 16th century, it features a massive *retablo* with various biblical scenes, and a gallery with an impressive organ. Jorge Oteiza's wonderfully fluid, modern *Pietá* stands outside the southern door.

La Bretxa
This modern complex lies at the point where the besieging English and Spanish forces entered the city during the Peninsular War – the name means 'the breach'. The main attraction is the underground food market, with fish, in particular, of spectacular quality.

Centro and New Town

Playa de la Concha

This beautiful curving strip of sand, has made San Sebastián what it is. Named *La Concha* (shell) for its shape, it gets seriously crowded in summer but is relatively quiet at other times, when the chilly water makes swimming a matter of bravado. Behind the beach, and even more emblematic, is the **Paseo**, a promenade barely changed from the golden age of seaside resorts. It's still the place to take the sea air and is backed by gardens, a lovely old merry-go-round, and a row of desirable beachfront hotels and residences that still yearn for the days when royalty strolled the shore every summer season.

Isla Santa Clara

Out in the bay this is a pretty rocky island that could have been placed there purposely as a feature. There's nothing on it but a lighthouse and a jetty, but it's prime picnic territory and the setting is unbeatable. It's only accessible by public transport during the summer, when a motorboat leaves from the harbour close to the end of the beach.

Ondarreta

Where the beach of La Concha graciously concedes defeat at a small rocky outcrop, the beach of Ondarreta begins. This is a good place to stay in summer, with less hustle and bustle. Atop the rock sits the **Palacio de Miramar**; commissioned by the regent María Cristina in the late 19th century, it would not look out of place offering bed and breakfast in an English village.

The **beach** of Ondarreta gazes serenely across at the rest of San Sebastián from beyond the Palacio de Miramar. It's a fairly exclusive and genteel part of town, appropriately watched over by a statue of a very regal Queen María Cristina. The beach itself feels somewhat more spacious than La Concha and, at the end the town, gives way to the jagged rocky coastline of Guipúzcoa. Integrating the two is *El Peine del Viento*, the comb of the wind, one of sculptor Eduardo Chillida's (see page 55) signature works. It consists of three twisted rusty iron whirls, which, at times, seem to be struggling to tame the ragged breezes that can sweep the bay. After a vain attempt to borrow helicopters to place the sculptures, the task was finally accomplished using a specially designed floating bridge.

Monte Igueldo

Above Ondarreta rises the steep Monte Igueldo, which commands excellent views of all that is San Sebastián. It's not a place to meditate serenely over the panorama – the summit of the hill is capped by a luxury hotel and a slightly tacky **amusement park** ① *€1.80 entrance by road*. The view makes it special though, and is unforgettable in the evening, when the city's lights spread out like a breaking wave below.

There's a **funicular** ① *1100-2000, €1.45/2.60 return*, running from a station behind the tennis club at the end of the beach. Otherwise it's a walk up the winding road beside it, which gives occasional views both ways along the coast. To reach Ondarreta and the funicular, walk or take bus No 16 from Plaza Guipúzcoa.

Catedral del Buen Pastor

The simple and elegant neo-Gothic Catedral del Buen Pastor is light and airy with an array of geometric stained glass, but in reality, there's little to detain the visitor – it's more impressive outside than in. Lovers of kitsch art will, however, have a field day – the Christ with sheep above the altar is upstaged by the painted choirboy with donation box in hand.

Gros

A bit more down-to-earth and relaxed than the rest of San Sebastián, Gros lies across the river and backs a good beach, which sees some decent surf. It's dominated by the Kursaal, but is also worth exploring for its off-the-beaten-track *pintxo* bars.

Kursaal
ⓘ *Av Zurriola 1, T943 003 000, www.kursaal.org, guided tours Fri-Sun 1330, €2.*
In a space that was derelict for three decades since the old Kursaal was demolished, these two stunning glass prisms opened their doors in 1999. Designed by Navarran architect Rafael Moneo to harmonize with the river mouth, the sea and 'communicate' with the hills of Uría and Urgull to either side, the concert hall has inspired much comment. The architect fondly refers to his building as 'two stranded rocks' – critics might agree – but the overall reaction has been very positive, and in 2001 the building won the European Union prize for contemporary architecture. The main building hosts concerts and conventions, while its smaller sidekick is an attractive exhibition centre. It's also the new home of the San Sebastián Film Festival and it houses a café and an upmarket modern restaurant as well. The Kursaal looks at its most impressive when reflecting the setting sun, or when lit up eerily at night.

Around San Sebastián

Museo Chillida-Leku
ⓘ *Ctra Hernani-Rekalde, T943 336 006, www.museochillidaleku.com, Sep-Jun daily 1030-1500, Jul-Aug Mon-Sat 1030-2000, Sun 1030-1500, €8.50, under-12s free.*
The Museo Chillida-Leku is a very relaxing place to spend a few hours out of the city. The late Basque sculptor Eduardo Chillida (see box, page 55) gracefully restored a 16th-century farmhouse with his own concepts of angles and open interior space. The lower floor, lit by a huge window, has a selection of large pieces; upstairs is some of his smaller, earlier work, as well as preparatory drawings. Around the house is a large park, which has about 40 of his larger sculptures (these are changeable depending on exhibition commitments). It's a very peaceful and shady place to stroll; the organized should pack a picnic. Bus No G2 from Calle Oquendo runs to the museum every 30 minutes on the half-hour.

Cider houses
ⓘ *The tourist office in San Sebastián has a map and list of the cider houses, several are in very picturesque locations with walking trails through the hills and valleys from Astigarraga and Hernani, a 15-min bus ride from Plaza Guipúzcoa in the centre.*
In the hills around Hernani and Astigarraga a short way south of town, apples are grown among stunning green hills. Although it's not hugely popular as a day-to-day drink in San Sebastián these days, cider has an important place in Guipúzcoan history. It's nothing like your mass-produced commercial ciders, being sharpish, yeasty and not very fizzy. It's best drunk fresh, poured from a height to give it some bounce after hitting the glass. The cider is mostly made in the hills in the many small *sagardotegiak*, or *sidrerías*. When it's ready, in early January, cider houses stoke up their kitchens, dust down the tables and fling the doors open to the Donostian hordes, who spend whole afternoons eating massive traditional cider house meals and serving themselves freely from taps on the side of the vats. It's an excellent experience even if you're not sold on the cider itself. Tradition has it that this lasts until late April or so, although several are now open year-round.

The typical meal served starts with *tortilla de bacalao* (salt-cod omelette), continues with a massive slab of grilled ox, and concludes with cheese, walnuts, and *membrillo* (quince jelly, delicious with the cheese). The best of the places are the simpler rustic affairs with long, shared, rowdy wooden tables and floors awash with the apple brew, but these tend to be harder to get to. Expect to pay from €15-30 for the *menú sidrería*, which includes as much cider as you feel like sinking.

Inland from San Sebastián → *For listings see pages 59-67.*

Guipúzcoa is crisscrossed by valleys that are lush from rainfall and dotted with small towns, some agricultural centres for the surrounding farmland, some seats of heavier Basque industry such as cement or paper manufacture.

In many ways this is the 'real' Basqueland and the smaller, poorer communities are still where separatism flourishes most strongly. The valleys also conceal beautiful churches (as well as the massive Loiola basilica), and plenty of walks and picnic spots. Due to Euskadi's good transport connections, many of these places are within easy day-trip range of both San Sebastián and Bilbao. However, there are good accommodation options, especially in *casas rurales* or *agroturismos*, usually Basque farmhouses with good welcoming accommodation in the heart of the countryside.

Santuario de Loiola → *Colour map 3, B3.*
Now here's a strange one. A massive **basilica** ① *Tue-Sat 1000-1230, 1500-1815, Sun 1000-1230, €2, best time to visit is during the week as at weekends it's overcrowded with pilgrims,* not quite St Peter's or St Paul's but not very far off, standing in the middle of Guipúzcoan pasture land. All is explained by the fact that St Ignatius, founder of the Jesuits (see page 70) was born here. The house where he first saw daylight has bizarrely had the basilica complex built around it; it's now a museum.

The most arresting feature of the basilica from a distance is the massive dome, which stands 65 m high. Designed by Carlo Fontana, an Italian architect from Bernini's school, it's topped by an ornate cupola. Lavish is the word to describe the rest of the decoration of the church; minimalist gurus will probably drop dead on the spot. The building is designed to be viewed from a distance – this is the function of the formal promenade in front of it – and what first strikes the visitor are the harmonious proportions. On closer inspection, the intricacy of the decoration becomes apparent. Inside, the baroque style is grandiose (almost to the point of pomposity), with a silver-plated statue of Ignatius himself gazing serenely at some very elaborate stonework and massive slabs of marble.

Those with a keen interest in the saint might want to take themselves down to nearby **Azpeitia** to see the font where he was baptized, in the church of San Sebastián.

Oñati → *Colour map 3, B2.*
The town of Oñati is one of the most attractive in the region and has a proud history as a university town and, until the mid-19th century, as a semi-independent fief of the local lord. The university, **Universidad de Sancti Spiritus**, was established in 1540 and is a beautiful example of cultured Renaissance architecture with an attractive colonnaded quadrangle. The stately red-balconied **Casa Consistorial** overlooks the main square where the two principal pedestrian streets, Calle Zaharra and Calle Barria, meet. These streets are the centre of the lively weekend nightlife as well as being the town's major axes. Oñati's **tourist office** is on Plaza de los Fueros.

Santuario de Arantzazu

Some 9 km south of Oñati is the Franciscan Santuario de Arantzazu, perching on a rock in a valley of great natural beauty. The basilica, built in the 1950s, is one of the most remarkable buildings in Euskadi. Incredibly avant-garde for the time, its spiky stone exterior is a reference to the hawthorn bush: according to tradition, a statue of Mary was found by a shepherd in 1468 on the spines of a hawthorn. A tinkling cowbell had led him to the spot, and the discovery ended years of war and famine in the area. The statue now sits above the altar, surrounded by the visionary abstract altarpiece of Luzio Muñoz. Although it appears to be made of stone, it's actually treated wood, and 600 sq m of it at that. Above the iron doors, sculpted by Eduardo Chillida, are Jorge Oteiza's fluid apostles and *Pietá*. He created great controversy by sculpting 14 apostles; for years they lay idle near the basilica as the Vatican wouldn't permit them to be erected. In the crypt, the impressive paintings of Néstor Basterretxea also caused problems with the church hierarchy. He originally painted the crucifixion backwards; when this was censured, he agreed to repaint it but with an angry Jesus. He succeeded – his powerful red Christ is an imposing figure. See box, page 55, for further information on Oteiza and Chillida.

There are some excellent opportunities for walking in the area, which is one of the most beautiful parts of Euskadi.

San Sebastián/Donostia listings

For Sleeping and Eating price codes and other relevant information, see pages 12-19.

🛏 Sleeping

San Sebastián *p50, map p52*
The Parte Vieja is the best spot for budget accommodation, with an unbelievable number of *pensiones*, some quite luxurious; there's also some near the cathedral around C San Martín. All accommodation in San Sebastián is overpriced; there is no getting away from the fact. High season is Jun-Sep; prices are at least 30% lower in most places outside this period. In the Kursaal, there's an office of Nekatur, which has a large portfolio of rural accommodation in the Basque lands. Be aware that the pedestrianized part of the old town can be extremely noisy at night, especially at weekends.
€€€€ Hotel de Londres y de Inglaterra, C Zubieta 2, T943 440 770, www.hlondres. com. Grand old beachfront hotel that is an emblem of the city's glory days. The rooms could do with a refit, but it's all about the location here. If royalty don't drop by as often as they once did, no one's letting

on. Spend the extra for a room with the stunning bay view, but consider elsewhere if you can't find a discounted rate online.
€€€€ Hotel María Cristina, C Oquendo 1, T943 437 600, www.starwoodhotels. com. Taking up an entire block, its elegant sandstone bulk has cradled more celebrities than you could drop a fork at. It has all the services, luxury, and style you would expect, including a child-minding service and a proper concierge, as well as prices that boot other Basque hotels into the campsite class. A double costs about €450 in summer, a bit more with views.
€€€€ Villa Soro, Av de Ategorrieta 61, T943 297 970, www.villasoro.com. To the east of Gros, this sumptuous 19th-century villa is something of an oasis, set in large grounds with manicured gardens. It really feels like a rural hotel, with discreet service, a refined, relaxing feel, and seriously comfortable rooms, some in an annexe. No restaurant (but wonderful Arzak is a short walk away). Free bikes offer a good way to zip around town. Recommended.
€€€€ Mercure Monte Igueldo, Paseo del Faro 134, T943 210 211, www.

monteigueldo.com. It's all about the view here: the hotel itself needs a bit of a refit. Right at the top of Monte Igueldo, most of the hotel's rooms offer spectacular vistas towards town or west along the coast. It's not really walking distance from the old centre though, and you can feel a bit isolated. There are often good special offers on booking websites.

€€€ Hotel Niza, C Zubieta 56, T943 426 663, www.hotelniza.com. Right on the beach, this hotel is an odd mixture of casual seaside and starchy formality. About half the comfortable, modernized rooms have views – but you can't book these ahead – the others face the road and can be a little noisy. The singles are a little dark but offer very good value.

€€€ Hotel Ezeiza, Av Satrustegui 13, Ondarreta, T943 214 311, www.hotelezeiza. com. Well situated at the peaceful western end of Ondarreta beach, this is a welcoming place with the added attraction of an excellent terrace bar.

€€€ Pensión Gran Bahía Bernardo, C Embeltrán 16, T943 420 216, www. pensiongranbahiabernardo.com. This attractive and upmarket *pensión* is convenient for both the beach and Parte Vieja. Recently renovated, the beds are very comfortable, and the rooms well equipped, a/c and quietish. There are a few different room categories. **€€** off-season.

€€ Hostal Alemana, C San Martín 53, T943 462 544, www.hostalalemana.com. An efficient modern *hostal* with warm personal service and a location just seconds away from the beach. Despite its *hostal* category it is effectively a hotel, with all the conveniences, plus some nice views and a pretty breakfast room. Minimum 5-night stay in Aug. It's **€€-€** off season.

€€ Pensión Edorta, C Puerto 15, T943 423 773, www.pensionedorta.com. Overpriced but charming, this beautiful *pensión* is right in the old town near the fishing harbour. Recently opened, with beautiful rooms with rough stone-faced walls, polished floorboards and elegant iron-headed beds. The bathrooms are also very elegant, but some are shared (**€€-€**).

€€ Pensión Aída, C Iztueta 9, Gros, T943 327 800, www.pensionesconencanto. com. A very good place to stay in Gros, and convenient for the station. The gleaming rooms are appealing, and the breakfast in bed is a great way to start the day. There's free Wi-Fi and internet, and they rent bikes.

€€ Pensión Altair, C Padre Larroca 3, T943 293 133, www.pension-altair.com. Gleaming, friendly, and with a decent location in Gros, this stylish and comfortable choice takes the humble *pensión* to stratospheric levels. With modern conveniences like free Wi-Fi, swipe cards and safes in the rooms, decorated with a soft contemporary scheme, this is one of the city's best. Book it ahead. Recommended.

€€ Pensión Bellas Artes, C Urbieta 64, T943 474 905, www.pension-bellasartes.com. A 15-min walk from the old town, this ultra-friendly *pensión* is well located for the bus and train stations, and easily found if arriving by car. The stylish rooms offer excellent comfort for this price. Recommended.

€€ Pensión Kursaal, C Peña y Goñi 2, T943 292 666, www.pensionesconencanto.com. A good place to stay just across the river in Gros, and very near the beach. The attractive rooms have large windows, bathrooms and TV. As in many of these old buildings, the plumbing and heating can make a racket. Internet access in the lobby and free Wi-Fi. Parking available under the Kursaal for €12 a day – a good deal. Recommended.

€€ Izar Bat, C Fermín Calbetón 6, T943 431 573, www.pensionizarbat.com. Kitted out in warm colours and with bathrooms so bright and clean you need sunglasses, this is a top Parte Vieja option. High beds are extremely comfortable, there are great modern facilities and a fridge in every room, and the front rooms are double glazed to avoid the worst of the noise. Recommended.

€€ Pensión San Martín, C San Martín 10, T943 428 714, www.pensionsanmartin.com.

One of the better of the host of choices on this street. The rooms are good and comfy, and have bathrooms and TV. Very handy for the train station. Free Wi-Fi.

€€-€ Pensión Amaiur, C 31 de Agosto 44, T943 429 654, www.pensionamaiur. com. Situated in the oldest house in the Parte Vieja (few others survived the 1813 fire), this is one of the best budget options in town. Lovingly decorated and sympathetically run, there's a variety of smallish but homely rooms, most with satellite TV and some with balconies. Guests have free use of the pretty (stoveless) kitchen, and there's coin-operated high-speed internet access and free Wi-Fi. Highly recommended.

€€-€ Pensión San Lorenzo, C San Lorenzo 2, T943 425 516, www.pensionsanlorenzo.com. A friendly star of the old town near the Bretxa market. The 5 well-priced rooms are brightly decorated and come with full bathroom, TV, fridge, kettle and piped radio. Internet access and Wi-Fi. It's a quiet place and highly recommended, but fills very fast. € off-season.

Camping

Camping Igueldo, Paseo Padre Orkolaga 69, T943 214 502, www.campingigueldo. com. Open all year, this big San Sebastián campsite is back from Ondarreta beach behind Monte Igueldo. They've got bungalows, and it's easily accessed on bus No 16 from near the tourist office.

Santuario de Loiola *p58*

€€ Hotel Loiola, Av de Loiola s/n, Loiola, T943 151 616, www.hotelloiola.com. Although the building itself won't win many prizes for harmonious rural architecture, it's handy for the basilica, and reasonable value. The rooms are a touch dull but don't lack conveniences.

€ Laja, Santa Cruz, Azkoitia, T943 853 075. A good choice on the edges of Azkoitia in a traditional-looking *baserri* farmhouse that offers home-cooked meals and very good-value rooms in striking distance of the basilica.

Oñati *p58*

The cheaper beds in Oñati fill up quickly at weekends.

€€ Ongi Etorri, C Zaharra 19, T943 718 285. This family-run hotel is well located on the main pedestrian street. The rooms are thoughtfully decorated, a touch small, but snug with heating and a/c.

€ Arregi, Ctra Garagaltza-Auzoa 21, T943 780 824, www.nekatur.net/arregi. An excellent *agroturismo* a couple of kilometres from Oñati. A big farmhouse in a green valley with beautiful dark-wood rooms, a ping-pong table, and pleasant owners. You can use the kitchen, or they can provide dinner with advance notice. Recommended.

€ Etxebarría, C Barria 15, T943 780 460. A cheap *pensión* not far from the main square. Rooms are clean and good value but it's definitely worth ringing ahead. It can get a little noisy at weekends.

Santuario de Arantzazu *p59*

There are a couple of hotels and restaurants in Arantzazu but, happily, nothing else.

€€ Hotel Santuario de Arantzazu, Arantzazu 29, T943 781 313, www. hotelsantuariodearantzazu.com. Right next to the basilica, this monk-run guesthouse has recently been converted to a modern hotel with spa and conference facilities. It's all very comfortable, but the restaurant leaves a bit to be desired. Great location.

❷ Eating

San Sebastián *p50, map p52*

San Sebastián is the gourmet capital of Spain, with some seriously classy restaurants dotting the city and the hills around. Several of the nation's finest eateries are here; as well as those we list, **Akelarre** (www. akelarre.net), **Martín Berasategui** (www. martinberasategui.com) and **Mugaritz** (www.mugaritz.com) are gourmet temples in and around town. It's also a great place for crawling around bars eating *pintxos*; the best zone for this is the Parte Vieja, where 'eat street' is **C Fermín Calbetón**, with several excellent places. **Gros** is a quieter but equally tasty option. Cold *pintxos* are arranged on the bartops here, but most places offer hot ones cooked to order. These can be a real highlight – look out for the board listing them. To order, get a waiters attention and say, for example, 'dos de foie' (2 foie *pintxos*). *Pintxos* cost €2.50-4. Eating in the city is far from cheap by Spanish standards. If you're here in spring, make sure you make a trip into the hills to one of the many cider houses (*sagardotegiak*) around the towns of Hernani and Astigarraga for no-frills good cheer, eating, and drinking. See www.sagardotegiak.com for a list of these establishments.

Arzak, Alto de Miracruz 21, T943 278 465, www.arzak.info. On a hill in the eastern reaches of town, this is many foodies' choice as Spain's top restaurant and it doesn't disappoint. The Arzak family has been running it for over a century, and it maintains some of that traditional atmosphere; it's no aloof gastronomic Parnassus, though the interior is darkly contemporary. The quality and innovation doesn't come cheap though. The degustation menu (€155 plus drinks) is the way to go here. Highly recommended.

Bodegón Alejandro, C Fermín Calbetón 4, T943 427 158. This popular spot has a homely, unpretentious interior; the focus is on the quality cuisine, which draws influences both from the new Basque wave and from upmarket French bistro traditions. Eating is via a bistro menu, which costs €37, and might see you follow crab ravioli with roast trotters. Drinks are extra.

Rekondo, Paseo de Igueldo 57, T943 212 907, www.rekondo.com. On the slopes of the Igueldo hill, with great views, this offers traditional but upmarket Basque cuisine that includes excellent grilled meats and well-treated fish. The real highlight is the wine cellar. With some 100,000 bottles, this is one of the nation's top wine collections.

Zuberoa, Barrio Iturriotz 8, T943 491 228, www.zuberoa.com. Outside San Sebastián, near the town of Oiartzun/Oyarzun is the lair of top chef Hilario Arbelaitz, in an attractive stone farmhouse with a wooden porch and terrace. Arbelaitz combines an essential Basqueness with a treatment inspired by the very best of French and Mediterranean cuisine. Everything is delicious, from a typical fish soup to the untypical grapefruit, spider crab and trout roe jelly with potato and olive oil cream. The degustation menu (€115) focuses on flavour more than fanciness and is a memorable feast.

A Fuego Negro, C 31 de Agosto, www. afuegonegro.com. Darkly modish and moody in red and black, this bar has become one of Donostia's in-vogue eating options. A bewildering mixture of Euskara and Spanish covers the blackboard – ask the waiter to recommend something or for the English translation if you're not sure what they're on about. The *pintxo* combinations are incredibly imaginative; they don't all work but you can have fun trying. Pricier than most.

Astelena, C Euskal Herría 3, T943 426 867, www.restauranteastelena.com. In a quiet side street near the Bretxa market, this modern place buzzes with chat during the week, when its €24 *menú* (available lunch Tue-Fri and dinner Tue-Thu), using fresh market produce, pulls in the punters. It offers excellent value for its stylish cuisine at any time.

Barbarin, C Puerto 21, T943 421 886, www.restaurantebarbarin.com. It's not gourmet, but this old-fashioned, friendly, comfortable and spacious restaurant specializes in well-priced seafood and rices. The *rollitos de txangurro* (fried crab rolls) are especially tempting; they also do a good paella (€40 for 2) and cheap steaks as well as various set menus from €20 a head.

Casa Urola, C Fermín Calbetón 20, T943 423 424. An enticing choice whether for *pintxos* or a full meal, this small and busy bar has exquisite gourmet snacks on the counter. There are 2 dining areas; upstairs is more peaceful. The fish dishes are excellent and the *solomillo*'s tasty too. Recommended.

¶¶ Ganbara, C San Jerónimo 21, T943 422 575. This is a fairly upmarket tapas bar and *asador* with a worthwhile array of *pintxos* to accompany the cheerfully poured wine. The *raciones* are delicious, with such delicacies as *trufas* (truffles) and *percebes* (goose barnacles) making an appearance.

¶¶ La Fábrica, C Puerto 17, T943 432 110, www.restaurantelafabrica.es. If *pintxo*-hopping is all getting a bit much and you want a sit-down meal without sacrificing quality or maxing out the credit card, head here. A good-quality set menu is only €25 lunch or dinner during the week (€38 at weekends), and is accompanied by friendly service in this stylishly appointed but comfortable space.

¶¶ Munto, C Fermín Calbeton 17, T943 426 088. This thoroughly worthwhile place is one of many good choices on this street. The downstairs *comedor* is very attractively lit and decorated, the service is attentive, and the food – tasty steaks and delicately-treated seafood – is of excellent quality for the price.

¶¶ Oquendo, C Oquendo 8, T943 420 932. A good, fairly formal restaurant near the **Hotel María Cristina**, serving a range of fresh fish around €18 a plate. It's a fine option at any time though, for there's a range of breakfasty pastries and tortillas, fine bar-top *pintxos*, and oysters and champagne for special occasions. The photo wall from the San Sebastián Film Festival is great for testing your silver-screen knowledge.

¶¶ Petritegi, Astigarraga s/n, T943 457 188, www.petritegi.com. In the cidery hills near town, this is one of the few *sagardotegiak* (cider house) to open year-round. The traditional cod omelette is excellent, and you pour your own cider straight from the barrel. The set menu is €28. It's open for dinner only, and lunch at weekends.

¶¶ Urepel, Paseo Salamanca 3, T943 424 040. A long and brooding restaurant with a fairly Spanish feel. The food is lighter,

and the highlight is an elegantly treated shellfish. A good wine list accompanies the classy nosh.

¶ Borda Berri, C Fermín Calbetón 12, T943 425 638, www.bordaberri.com. The checked tiles and *pintxo*-free wooden bar make it feel like you've stepped into another country suddenly. But once you get your lips around the melt-in-the-mouth foie, the slow-cooked duck magret, or the carrilleras, you're back in gourmet heaven. All prepared to order. Recommended.

¶ Bar Gorriti, C San Juan 3, T943 428 353. An unglamorous bar that's been going since the 1920s. Somewhat surprisingly, on entering you are confronted with a mighty impressive spread of cold *pintxos* during the day and early evening. You could spend all day in here if you weren't careful. A great spot and an antidote to the overelaboration in some of the newer places.

¶ Bar Ondarra, Av de la Zurriola 16, T943 326 033. Opposite the Kursaal exhibition centre in Gros, this is a no-frills tapas bar with a small street level and an underground den featuring regular live jazz and soul. Good cold *pintxos*.

¶ Casa Gandarias, C 31 de Agosto 25, T943 428 106. This busy tapas bar is near the Santa María church and has an adjoining restaurant. The *pintxos* are excellent and are served by efficient and cordial staff. The *solomillo* or the grilled foie are particularly recommended. Good whisky selection, too.

¶ Casa Vergara, C Mayor 21, T943 431 073. This highly recommendable tapas bar is on the corner of the ever-popular 31 de Agosto. While it's worth sitting down in the simple but comfortable *comedor* to try *raciones* of stews like *callos* (tripe), *chipirones* (squid) or *pulpo* (octopus), the *pintxos* at the bar are delightful. Try the *gulas* wrapped in smoked salmon if they're about. It's well priced too.

¶ Garbola, Paseo Colón 11, T943 285 019. Legendary for its scrumptious mushroom creations and *caipirinhas*, this Gros bar also offers more unusual snacks, such as kangaroo and shark. It's very plush and old-fashioned inside.

Goiz Argi, C Fermín Calbetón 4, T943
425 204. A warmly welcoming family-run
place, this specializes in skewered *pintxos*.
The hot ones are very tasty: prawns with a
spicy garlic and chilli sauce might have you
ordering seconds.

La Cepa, C 31 de Agosto 7, T943 426 394.
Perennially and deservedly popular tapas
bar lined with hams and featuring the head
of a particularly large *toro* on the wall. You
can eat better in other places, but a good
atmosphere is guaranteed here..

La Cuchara de San Telmo, C 31 de Agosto
28 (back), T943 420 840. An extraordinary
bar up the side of the museum. The
Cuchara's tiny open kitchen pioneered the
idea of *pintxos* in the form of made-to-
order gourmet dishes in miniature, now
something found in several of Donostia's
bars. There's a short, changing menu, but
everything is delicious. It's an inspiring and
down-to-earth place. Highly recommended.

Portaletas, C Puerto 8, T943 423 888.
This welcoming establishment offers
unpretentious hospitality, with its stone-
faced walls and wooden beams. There are
appetizing *pintxos*, mostly on slices of bread.
There's also a cheap *menú del día* and good
value *raciones* (€5-10).

Tamboril, C Pescadería 2, T943 423 507.
San Sebastián's pretty plaza is largely devoid
of appealing bars, but this smart little spot
partly redresses that. Quality gourmet
pintxos and decent wines served politely
make it a worthwhile stop. Just watch your
glass on the rickety wooden rests. There's a
pleasant terrace on the square in summer.

Txepetxa, C Pescadería 5, T943 422 227.
Nobody seems to like anchovies any more,
but you'll like these: the fresh kind, not the
salted ones. They come in myriad ways,
advertised by lifelike plastic models. With
foie gras and apple? Doesn't sound like it'd
work, but it does.

Zeruko, C Pescadería 10. Don't mind the
sawdust on the floor, this is a very smart bar
that produces *pintxos* and *raciones* of the

highest class. The main dishes are based
around stew-type meals, with *chipirones en
su tinta* (squid in ink) particularly delicious.
The bar snacks are so elaborate you'll have
to ask what most of them are.

Cafés

Café de la Concha, Paseo de la Concha
s/n, T943 473 600. A pretty place to stop
for a coffee or a glass of wine during a
stroll along the beach. It's also got a decent
restaurant with good views and a terrace.
€13 *menú del día*, a euro more if you eat
outside.

Iturralde, Av Libertad 11, T943 428 690. You
might struggle to squeeze into this narrow
spot, but it's worth it. There's really excellent
coffee and teas and infusions bursting
with flavour. The owner knows what she's
doing, so if she suggests something say yes.
Recommended.

Ni Neu, Av Zurriola 1, T943 003 162. The
outdoor part of this Kursaal restaurant is an
excellent spot for an early evening *pintxo*
and drink, with superb views over the river
mouth and sea.

Santuario de Loiola *p58*

Kiruri, Loiola Auzoa 24, T943 815 608,
www.kiruri.com. The best option in the area,
directly opposite the basilica. It does some
good traditional dishes and is popular for its
rabas (calamari strips). Service can be slow if
there's a coachload of pilgrims in. There's a
good terrace outside.

Oñati *p58*

The **Etxebarría** (see Sleeping, above) runs
a good cheap restaurant a couple of doors
down the street. The **Zelai-Zabal** (www.
zelaizabal.com) in Arantzazu has a sound
reputation.

Bars and clubs

San Sebastián *p50, map p52*
The Parte Vieja has many options and the
crossroads of C Larramendi and C Reyes

Católicos near the cathedral is full of bars. There's studenty nightlife around **C San Bartolomé**, just back from the beach.

Altxerri Bar, C Reina Regenta 2, www. altxerri.com. An atmospheric cellar bar by the tourist office that regularly showcases live jazz and other acts. Draws an interesting crowd and is worthwhile even if there's nothing on. Open 1700 to late.

Bataplán, Playa de la Concha s/n, T943 460 439, www.bataplandisco.com. San Sebastián's most famous *discoteca*, right on La Concha beach. Open Thu-Sat from 2400 and attracts a smart young crowd. The music is mostly club anthems and pop crowd pleasers. Rises to prominence during the film festival when it hosts various after-parties. €7-15 entry.

Be Bop, Paseo de Salamanca 3. This well-visited bar by the river mouth is quiet and relaxing and has regular live jazz music playing; entry is usually about €5.

Bideluze, Plaza Guipúzcoa 14, T943 422 880. A lively and interesting bar, with 2 floors of eccentric furniture, on the south side of Plaza Guipúzcoa. Simple food is served downstairs and *pintxos* upstairs. It's popular with young and old; you may be addressed in Euskara.

El Nido, C Larramendi 13. A sizeable pub that fills after work and doesn't empty again until late. Friendly crowd and board games.

Garagar, Alameda del Boulevard 22, T943 422 840. Slightly overpriced pub at the edge of the Parte Vieja with some comfy booths. Busy till 0200 most nights (0400 at weekends), and more relaxed than some of the other late openers. There's a DJ upstairs at weekends.

Komplot, C Pedro Egaña 5, T943 472 109, www.komplot.es. Small and fashionable club featuring probably the best house music in San Sebastián.

Mendaur, C Fermín Calbetón 8, T943 422 268. Crowded and lively, this Parte Vieja spot packs them in every night with frequent drink specials. If you're looking for the action on a quiet weeknight, it'll be here.

Museo del Whisky, Alameda Boulevard 5, T943 426 478. Elegant and refined, this 2-level bar does indeed have a sizeable whisky collection on shelves all around. The mixed drinks are pricy and delicious, and there's an atmosphere of well-heeled good cheer.

Rotonda, Playa de la Concha 6, T943 429 095, www.rotondadisco.com. Another club on La Concha beach and open very late weekend nights. The music hovers around popular dance, with some salsa and reggae thrown in as required.

Oñati *p58*

For later action, head for one of the bars on C Zaharri, such as **Bar Irritz**, which is friendly and has a popular techno scene at weekends.

⚙ Entertainment

San Sebastián *p50, map p52*
Bullfighting
Near the stadium is the bullring, **Illumbe**, which includes a massive cinema complex.

Football club

Estadio de Anoeta, Paseo de Anoeta 1, T943 462 833, www.real-sociedad-sad.es. This is the home of **Real Sociedad**, the city's football team. Given the title 'Real' (Royal) in 1910 by the king, who spent much time in the city, the club is one of comparatively few to have won the Spanish league title. Tickets €25-40 (sold at the stadium from the Thu afternoon before a game to the Sat evening, then 2 hrs before kick-off, usually 1700 on Sun).

Theatre

The beautiful **Teatro Victoria Eugenia** is a sparklingly atmospheric place to catch a show, and benefits greatly from its recent restoration. The box office, T943 481 818, www.victoriaeugenia.com, is open 1130-1330, 1700-2000; there's also a good café-restaurant.

⊛ Festivals and events

San Sebastián *p50, map p52*
19-20 Jan Tamborrada, the feast day of San Sebastián, is celebrated with a deafening parade of drummers through the streets from midnight on the 19th.
Week before 15 Aug Aste Nagusia or 'big week', the city's major fiesta, kicks off in San Sebastián with world-renowned fireworks exhibitions.
3rd week of Sep International Film Festival.

⊙ Shopping

San Sebastián *p50, map p52*
La Bretxa, Plaza de Bretxa, Market complex in the Old Town. The food market downstairs is the best bit.
Solbes, C Aldamar 4, T943 427 818. A delicatessen and wine shop with a high-quality, not particularly cheap line-up.
Zaporejai, C San Jerónimo 21, T943 422 882, www.zaporejai.com. In the old town, this place sells a variety of excellent hams. It's a friendly spot, and they'll be pleased to explain about piggy products and let you taste things.

▲ Activities and tours

San Sebastián *p50, map p52*
The tourist office hires out multilingual audio guides for the city; these cover the old town and cost €10 for a day. There's a hop-on, hop-off bus that runs Oct-Jun daily except Tue (mornings only in winter months), and daily Jul-Sep. Ticket (€12) valid for 24 hrs; another service goes to the Chillida museum. There's also a small tourist train (www.txu-txu.com) running around the streets. It leaves every hour from the corner of Miramar and Andia just behind the beach in the centre of town.
The boat *Ciudad San Sebastián*, T670 977 877, www.ciudadsansebastian.com, runs ½-hr trips around the bay, with hourly departures daily in summer and at weekends in spring and autumn, €8 (leaves from halfway along aquarium wharf).

San Sebastián Food, T634 759 503, www.sansebastianfood.com, is an excellent English-speaking set-up that offers various gourmet options from *pintxo* tours of the old town – a good way to get the hang of this sometimes intimidating way of eating – *pintxo* cookery classes, wine tastings, Rioja visits and more. You can book online. Recommended.

⊖ Transport

San Sebastián *p50, map p52*
Bicycle hire Bici Rent Donosti, Av de la Zurriola 22, T943 279 260, www.bicirentdonosti.galeon.com. Open daily 0900-2100, this shop on Gros beach rents bikes by the hour and by the day. They're not cheap at €18 per day, but there's a decent range, and the staff will help with planning trips. **Alai Txirrinduak**, Av Madrid 24, T943 470 001, www.alaitxirrinduak.com, and Grosgreen Bicicletas, C Peña y Goni 3, are other places to rent bikes.

Bus The main bus station is an inconvenient 20-min walk from the old town; buses No 26 and No 28 run there regularly from the Alameda del Boulevard. For the tickets, you have to go to the company offices, situated on Paseo Vizcaya and Av Sancho el Sabio on either side of the bus bays.
Bilbao (1 hr 20 mins, €10) is served at least hourly, and **Vitoria** (1 hr 40 mins, €8) 7 or more times a day.
Other destinations include **Pamplona** (8 daily, 1 hr 15 mins), **Madrid** (11 daily, 5 hrs 45 mins), **Burgos** (4 daily, 3-4 hrs), and **Santander** (9 daily, 3-4 hrs). There are also buses to **Bayonne** and **Biarritz** in France.
Shorter-haul buses to Guipúzcoan destinations leave from the central Plaza Guipúzcoa. Destinations include **Zumaia**, **Zarautz**, **Azkoitia** and **Loiola** (the exception; this leaves from the bus station), **Tolosa**, **Oiartzun**, **Hernani**, **Astigarraga**, all with very frequent departures.

Train There are mainline train departures to **Madrid** (3 daily, 5 hrs 30 mins, from €50) and other Spanish cities.

There are 7 trains a day for **Vitoria** (1 hr 40 mins, from €10). **Euskotren** connects the city with other Basque destinations on the coast and inland: its hub is Amara, on Plaza Easo in the south part of the new town. **Bilbao** is served hourly via the coast (2 hrs 40 mins). **El Topo** (the Mole) is a train service running from Amara to **Hendaye** in France, it runs every 10-15 mins and takes 35 mins. At Hendaye you can change to mainline SNCF train services.

Santuario de Loiola *p58*

Bus You can reach Azkoitia and Loiola by bus from **Bilbao's** bus station (3 a day), and from **San Sebastián** (hourly, 1 hr) (destination may be marked 'Azpeitia').

Oñati *p58*

Bus Oñati is accessed by bus from **Bilbao's** bus station with **Pesa** once daily Mon-Fri, otherwise connect with local bus from **Bergara**. There's no public transport from Oñati to Arantzazu; a taxi costs about €10 each way. Walking from Oñati takes about 2 hrs, but the return trip downhill is significantly quicker. There's plenty of traffic, and it's easy to hitch a ride.

Directory

San Sebastián *p50, map p52*

Internet and telephone Locutorio Puerto, C Puerto 14, cheap internet plus phone calls; Navinet, C Fermín Calbetón 11, in the heart of the old town. **Language courses** Lacunza, C Mundaiz 8, T943 326 680, www.lacunza. com; Tandem San Sebastián, C Pasajes 4, T943 326 705, www.tandemsansebastian. com. **Laundry** Wash'n Dry, C Iparragirre 6, San Sebastián, T943 293 150, is an Aussie laundromat across the river in Gros offering self-serve and drop-off facilities. **Medical services** Hospital Nuestra Señora de Arantzazu, Av Doctor Begiristain 115, T943 007 000. **Police** The emergency number for all necessities is T112, while T091 will take you to the local police. Policia Municipal San Sebastián, C Larramendi 10, T943 450 000, is the main police station. **Post office** C Urdaneta s/n.

Guipúzcoan Coast

Crossing the French border, the first stretches of Spain are well worth investigating, starting with the very first town. Hondarribia is a beautiful walled place completely free of the malaise that seems to afflict most border towns; if you don't mind a few day trippers, this is one of the most attractive towns in Euskadi. It's a good place to stay, but is easily reached as an excursion from San Sebastián too.

The coast west of San Sebastián is characterized by some fairly muscular cliffs interspersed with a few excellent beaches, a popular summer playground. As with Vizcaya, the area's history is solidly based on the fishing of anything and everything from anchovies to whales. While Zarautz's aim in life seems to be to try and emulate on a smaller scale its big brother San Sebastián just along the coast, Getaria is a particularly attractive little port.>> *For listings, see pages 90-74.*

East of San Sebastián → *For listings, see pages 90-74.*

Hondarribia/Fuenterrabia
This old fishing port sits at the mouth of the Río Bidasoa looking directly across at France, a good deal more amicably now than for much of its history. The well-preserved 15th-century walls weren't erected just for decoration, and the city has been besieged more times than it cares to remember.

Although there's a fishing port, very busy marina, and a decent beach, the most charming area of Hondarribia is the walled part, a hilly grid of cobbled streets entered through arched gates. The stone used for many of the venerable old buildings seems to be almost luminous in the evening sun. The hill is topped by a plaza and a 16th-century **palace of Carlos V**, now a parador; its imposing bulk is offset by a very pretty courtyard. Nearby, the **Iglesia de Santa María de Manzano** is topped by a belltower and an impressive coat-of-arms. It was here in 1660 that María Teresa, daughter of Felipe IV, married Louis XIV of France, the Sun King. **Plaza Guipúzcoa** is even nicer than the main square, with cobbles and small but ornate buildings overhanging a wooden colonnade.

Outside the walls, the marina is busy with yachts and sits at the river mouth, just behind the beach. It's worth exploring the headland beyond here. Passing the fishing harbour, you reach a lighthouse with spectacular views. Below here, the Asturiaga bay has some remains from its days as a Roman anchorage. Above it is a small fort, the Castillo de San Telmo, not open to the public.

Information is available from Hondarribia's **tourist office** ⓘ *C Ugarte 6, T943 645 458, www.bidasoaturismo.com, Oct-Jun Mon-Fri 0930-1330, 1600-1830, Sat-Sun 1000-1400, Jul-Sep daily 1000-1500, 1600-1900*. Hondarribia makes an excellent place to stay, with several appealing hotels.

Near Hondarribia, the town of **Irún** is joined by road and rail to **Hendaye** in France but has little of interest except **Museo Oiasso** ⓘ *Eskoleta 1, T943 639 353, www.oiasso.com, €4.50, Tue-Sun 1000-1400, 1600-1900 (2000 summer)*, attractively displaying finds from the ancient Roman settlement here of the same name.

Pasaia/Pasajes

West of Hondarribia, the GI-3440 rises steeply, affording some fantastic views over a long stretch of coastline. Between Hondarribia and San Sebastián, it's worth stopping at Pasaia/Pasajes, the name given to a group of towns clustering around a superb natural harbour 6 km east of San Sebastián. **Pasajes San Juan** (Pasai Donibane), distinct from the other parts that are devoted to large-scale shipbuilding, is a very charming town that literally only has one street, which wends its way along the water, twisting around some buildings and simply going through others. While now dwarfed by the industry across the water, this was for periods in history the most important Basque port. The Romans made use of it to export mining products; whaling expeditions boldly set off for some very far-flung destinations indeed; and a good part of the Spanish Armada was built and crewed from this area. A later boost was given to the town as a result of the chocolate trade with Venezuela but by the time Victor Hugo came to live here for a spell, it was no longer the shipping centre it had been.

Pasajes gets a fair number of French tourists strolling through, which means that there are several restaurants (although, at time of writing, no accommodation). Apart from eating and strolling, there's not much going on, although you might want to investigate **Ontziola** ⓘ *T943 494 521*, an organization that builds traditional Basque boats, such as were used in Pasajes' heyday. There's a **tourist office** ⓘ *daily 1100-1400, 1600-1800*, in Victor Hugo's old pad. Their website www.oarsoaldea-turismo.net gives ideas for activities in the area.

West of San Sebastián → *For listings, see pages 90-74.*

Zarautz

While similarly blessed with a beautiful stretch of sandy beach and a characterful old town, like its neighbour San Sebastián, Zarautz has suffered from quick-buck beachfront high-rise development, which seems to appeal to the moneyed set who descend here by the thousand during the summer months. Nevertheless, along with the rows of bronzed bodies and the prudish but colourful changing tents, it can be quite a fun place. There's a good long break for surfing – one of the rounds of the world championship is often held here – and there's scope for more unusual watersports such as windboarding.

The old town is separated from the beach by the main road, giving Zarautz a slightly disjointed feel. There are a few well-preserved medieval structures, such as the **Torre Luzea**, and a handful of decent bars. Zarautz is known for its classy restaurants; after all, there's more to a Basque beach holiday than fish 'n' chips. There is a **tourist office** ⓘ *Nafarroa Kalea s/n, T943 830 990, www.turismozarautz.com, winter Mon-Fri 0930-1300, 1530-1930, Sat 1000-1400, summer Mon-Sat 0900-2030, Sun 1000-1400*, on a modern square on the main street through town.

The army of Christ

There can be few organizations that have had such an impact on all levels of world history than the Society of Jesus, or Jesuits. Their incident-filled five centuries of existence matches the strange life of their founder, Iñigo de Loiola (see page 58), a Basque from a small town in the valleys of Guipúzcoa.

Born in 1491 to a wealthy family, Iñigo was the youngest of 13 children. Sent as a pageboy to the court of Castilla, he embarked on a life of gambling, womanizing and duelling. Fighting alongside his brother in an attempt to relieve the French siege of Pamplona, he was badly wounded in the legs by a cannonball. After being taken prisoner and operated on, he was sent home on a stretcher by the French, who admired his courage. His leg didn't mend, however, and it had to be rebroken and set. Although near to death several times, the bones eventually healed, but the vain Iñigo realized to his horror that a knob of bone still protruded from his leg, which had become shorter than the other. Desperate to strut his stuff as a dashing courtier again and despite anasthetics not being available, he ordered the doctors to saw the bone off and lengthen the leg by repeated stretching.

During the boredom and pain of his lengthy convalescence, he began to read the only books at hand, the lives of the saints and a book on Jesus. Finally recovered in 1522, he set off on a journey, hoping to reach Jerusalem. Not far from home, riding muleback, he came across a Moor, with whom he argued about the virginity of Mary in her later life. When they parted company at a fork in the road, Iñigo decided that if his mule followed the Moor, he would kill him, and if it went the

other way, he would spare him. Luckily the mule went the other way.

After further enlightening experiences, and a spell in jail courtesy of the Inquisition, Iñigo ended up in Paris, meditating on what later became his Spiritual Exercises. His sceptical roommate was Francis Xavier, another Basque, whom Iñigo eventually won over. He and some companions travelled to Rome and, with the Pope's blessing, formed the Society of Jesus.

Iñigo died in 1556 and was canonized along with Francis Xavier in 1609. Since then the Jesuits, 41 saints on, have shared his passion for getting their hands dirty, being involved in education, charity and, more ominously, politics. They are a favoured target of conspiracy theorists, who see them as the real power behind the Vatican – the top Jesuit, the Superior General, is often called the 'Black Pope.'

For many centuries, however, the Jesuits were the prime educational force in western Europe and the New World: they have been called the 'schoolmasters of Europe'. The *reducciones*, communities of native Amerindians that they set up in Paraguay and Argentina were a brave and enlightened attempt to counteract slavery. These efforts, made famous by the film *The Mission*, were lauded by Voltaire (an unlikely source of praise) as "a triumph of humanity which seems to expiate the cruelties of the first conquerors". As a direct result of these works they were expelled from South America and Spain. In more recent times, the Jesuits have again courted the displeasure of western powers by advocating human rights in South America, so-called liberation theology seen as a grave danger to US muscle power in the region.

Getaria/Guetaria

Perched on a hunk of angled slate, Getaria is well worth a stop en route between Bilbao and San Sebastián. Despite being a large-scale fish cannery, the town is picturesque with cobbled streets winding their way to the harbour and, bizarrely, through an arch in the side of the church.

Getaria gets its fair share of passing tourists, which is reflected in the number of *asadores* that line its harbour and old centre. For an unbeatable authentic local feed, order a bottle of sprightly local *txakoli* and wash it down with a plate of grilled sardines – you'll turn your nose up at the canned variety for ever more.

The **Iglesia de San Salvador** is intriguing, even without the road that passes under it. The wooden floor lists at an alarming angle; to the faithful in the pews the priest seems to be saying mass from on high.

You won't stay long without coming across a statue of **Juan Sebastián Elkano**, winner of Getaria's most famous citizen award for nearly 500 years running, although fashion designer Cristóbal Balenciaga has come close in more recent times. Elkano, who set sail in 1519 on an expedition captained by Magellan, took command after the skipper was murdered in the Philippines. Sailing into Sevilla with the scant remnants of the expedition's crew, he thus became the first to circumnavigate the world. Not a bad finish for someone who had mutinied against the captain only a few months after leaving port.

Beyond the harbour, the wooded hump of San Antón is better known as **El Ratón** (the mouse), for its resemblance to that rodent. There are good views from the lighthouse at its tip; if the weather is clear you can see the coast of France northwards on the horizon.

Behind Getaria, a country road winds its way into the hills through the vineyards of the local *txakoli* producers. It makes a pleasant stroll from town, rewarded with some spectacular coastal views.

Zumaia/Zumaya

Some 5 km further along, Zumaia is not as attractive, but has the worthwhile **Museo Zuloaga** ⓘ *Ctra San Sebastián-Bilbao, T943 862 341, Apr-Sep only, Wed-Sun 1600-2000*. Ignacio Zuloaga, born in 1870, was a prominent Basque painter and a member of the so-called 'Generation of 98', a group of artists and thinkers who symbolized Spain's intellectual revival in the wake of the loss of the Spanish-American War, known as 'the disaster'. Zuloaga lived in this pretty house and garden, which now contains a good portion of his work as well as other paintings he owned, including some Goyas, El Grecos and Zurbaráns. Zuloaga himself is most admired for his expressive portraiture, with subjects frequently depicted against a typically bleak Spanish landscape. In the best of his work, the faces of the painted have a deep wisdom and a deep sadness that seems to convey both the artist's love and hatred for his country. The museum is a 15-minute walk on the Getaria/San Sebastián road from the centre of Zumaia.

Guipúzcoan Coast listings

For Sleeping and Eating price codes and other relevant information, see pages 12-19.

☕ Sleeping

Hondarribia *p68*
€€€€ Parador de Hondarribia, Plaza de Armas 14, T943 645 500, www.parador.es.

This fortress was originally constructed in the 10th century, then reinforced by Carlos V to resist French attacks. Behind the beautiful façade is a hotel of considerable comfort and delicacy, although the rooms don't reach the ornate standard set by the public areas. A pretty courtyard and terrace are the highlights.

€€€€ Hotel Pampinot, C Mayor 5, T943 640 600, www.hotelpampinot.com. Behind a charming façade, this wonderfully restored *palacio* has added yet another immensely appealing place to stay in Hondarribia. The rooms, opulent and stylish, are charismatically and distinctively decorated, including whimsical ceiling frescoes to gaze at as you recline in the plush beds. The price (at the low end of this range) seems a bargain for this level of quality and service. Recommended.

€€€ Hotel Obispo, Plaza del Obispo s/n, T943 645 400, www.hotelobispo.com. The former archbishop's palace is also overflowing with character; it's a beautiful building and features some pleasant views across the Bidasoa. The rooms are delightful, particularly those on the top floor. Free internet access for guests and frequent special offers.

€€ Hotel Palacete, Plaza Guipúzcoa 5, T943 640 813, www.hotelpalacete.net. Winningly situated on Hondarribia's prettiest plaza, and with modern, compact rooms with a colourful, airy feel, this hotel offers good value and welcoming service in the heart of things. There's a pleasing garden patio for quiet moments.

€€ Hostal Txoko-Goxoa, C Murrua 22, T943 644 658, www.txokogoxoa.es. A pretty little place in a peaceful part of town by the town walls (enter from the street below). The bedrooms are on the small side but homely, with flowers in the window boxes, and spotlessly clean.

€€ Hostal Alvarez Quintero, C Bernat Etxepare 2, T943 642 299. A tranquil little place with a distinctly old-fashioned air. The rooms are simple but not bad for this price in this town. It's a little difficult to find: the entrance is through an arch on the roundabout by the tourist office.

Camping

Faro de Higuer, Paseo del Faro 58, T943 641 008, F640 150. 1 of 2 decent campsites, slightly closer to town on the way to the lighthouse. There's a pool, lively bar, and a few bungalows.

Zarautz *p69*

See also Eating, below.

€€ Pensión Txikipolit, Plaza Música s/n, T943 835 357, www.txikipolit.com. One of the nicest budget options. Very well located in a square in the old part of town, with comfy and characterful rooms with plenty of facilities including a popular restaurant. Significantly cheaper off season.

Camping

Gran Camping Zarautz, T943 831 238, www.grancampingzarautz.com. A massive campsite with the lot, open all year but packed in summer's dog days.

Getaria *p71*

€€ Pensión Katrapona, Plaza Katrapona s/n, T943 140 409, www.katrapona.com. Set in a great restored stone building tucked away behind the **Mayflower** restaurant, this upmarket modern *pensión* has spotless and comfortable rooms with plenty of natural light and little balconies.

€€ Hotel Itxas Gain, C San Roque 1, T943 141 033, www.hotelitxasgain.com. Lovely place overlooking the sea (that's what the name means). This warm-hearted and open place has some lovely rooms with impressionist pictures on the walls. On the top floor there's a suite with a spa-bath. There's also a garden, which is a top place to relax in hot weather, and a friendly dog.

€€ Pensión Iribar, C Nagusia 34, T943 140 451, iribarjatetxea@yahoo.com. Clean and comfy little rooms with bathroom around the back of the restaurant of the same name, right in the narrow heart of the old town.

€ Gure Ametsa, Orrua s/n, T943 140 077, www.caseriogureametsa.com. Off a backroad between Zumaia and Getaria, this friendly, simple rural accommodation is in a superb location with hilly views over the sea. There are also cheaper rooms without en suite.

🍴 Eating

Hondarribia *p68*

The town is notable for its excellent restaurants; the location between San Sebastián and France is propitious.

Alameda, C Minasoroeta 1, T943 642 789, www.restalameda.com. Pushing hard for the Hondarribia gold medal, this exquisite spot serves elaborate gourmet dishes with a confident, well-presented flair. The short menu is bolstered by appealing daily specials, and there are also 3 multi-course set menus to choose from.

Sebastián, C Mayor 9, T943 640 167, www.sebastianhondarribia.com. Closed during Nov and on Mon. This excellent restaurant is attractively set in a dingy old grocery packed with interesting aromas. The food goes far beyond the humble decor, with a good-value *menú de degustación*.

Bar Itxaropena, C San Pedro 67, T943 641 197. A good bar in the new town offering a variety of cheap foodstuffs and plenty of company at weekends. Turns into a pub later in the evening.

Zarautz *p69*

Karlos Arguiñano, C Mendilauta 13, T943 130 000, www.hotelka.com. This is the lair of Spain's most famous TV chef, a cheerful, almost ubiquitous fellow. Right on the beach, his restaurant, converted from a stone mansion, boasts high-class cuisine that's innovative without losing its local roots. There are also comfortable hotel rooms (**L** in summer) set in the tower of the building and great views over the beach from the castellated rooftop terrace.

Kulixka, C Bixkonde 1, T943 134 604. This is a welcoming waterfront restaurant with an unbeatable view of the beach. There's good seafood as you'd expect, roast meats and a decent *menú del día* for €12.90, as well as a night-time version for €18.

Getaria *p71*

Kaia-Kaipe, C Katrapona Aundia 10, T943 140 500, www.kaia-kaipe.com. The best and priciest of Getaria's restaurants with a sweeping view over the harbour and high standard of food and service. Whole fish grilled over the coals outside are a highlight, as is the exceptional and reasonable wine list. Try some of the local *txakolí*, the best around.

Mayflower, C Katrapona 4, T943 140 658. One of a number of *asadores* in this attractive harbour town, with the bonus of an excellent *menú del día*. Grilled sardines are a tasty speciality.

Politena, Kale Nagusia 9, T943 140 113. A bar oriented towards weekend visitors from Bilbao and San Sebastián. There's a very enticing selection of *pintxos*, and a €13.50 'weekend' *menú*, which isn't bad either.

Txalupa, C Herrierieta 1, T943 140 592. A great place to buy or taste the local fish and *txakolí* in a hospitable bar, which offers *pintxos* as well as *cazuelitas*, small portions of bubbling stews or seafood in sauce.

⛰ Activities and tours

Getaria *p71*
Diving
K-Sub, C Txoritonpe 34, T943 140 185, www.ksub.net. Offers PADI scuba courses, and hires out diving equipment. Also gives advice on good locations.

⊖ Transport

Hondarribia *p68*

Bus There are buses to and from Plaza Guipúzcoa in **San Sebastián** every 20 mins. A few buses cross the border into France. There are frequent buses linking Hondarribia with **Irún**, just a few kilometres down the road, from where there's more regular cross-border transport to neighbouring **Hendaye**.

Boat Boats run across the river to the French town of **Hendaye**.

Train The most common way of crossing the border is by the *topo* train that burrows through the mountain from between **San Sebastián** or **Irún** and **Hendaye**.

Zarautz *p69*
Bus Buses run regularly to/from **San Sebastián** bus station.

Train Zarautz is serviced by **Euskotren** hourly from **Bilbao's** Atxuri station and **San Sebastián**'s Amara station.

Getaria *p71*
Bus Getaria is serviced by bus from **San Sebastián** bus station regularly.
Train Zumaia is serviced by **Euskotren** trains hourly from **Bilbao**'s Atxuri station and San Sebastián's Amara station. Regular buses connect the two towns.

Vizcayan Coast

The Vizcayan section of the Basque coastline is some of the most attractive and dramatic of Northern Spain: cliffs plunge into the water around tiny fishing villages, surfers ride impossibly long breaks, and the towns, like spirited Ondarroa, are home to a convivial and quintessentially Basque social scene. The eastern section is the most rough-edged, with stirring cliffs and startling geological folding contrasting with the green foliage. Fishing is god around here: some of the small villages are far more accessible by sea than by land. The main town of this stretch is Lekeitio, one of Euskadi's highlights. » *For listings, see pages 99-83.*

Ondarroa → *For listings, see pages 87-90.*

The friendliest of towns, Ondarroa marks the border of Vizcaya and Guipúzcoa. Situated at the mouth of the Río Artibai, the town is straddled by two bridges, one the harmonious stone **Puente Viejo**, the other a recent work by Santiago Calatrava, which sweeps across with unmistakable panache. Although low on glamour and short on places to stay, Ondarroa could be worth a stop if you're exploring the coast, particularly on a Friday or Saturday night, when the nightlife rivals anywhere in Euskal Herría.

Music has long been a powerful vehicle of Basque expression, and here the bars pump not with salsa or *bacalao* but nationalist rock.

Markina-Xemein

This village in the Vizcayan hills, a short distance inland from Ondarroa, is set around a long leafy plaza. Not a great deal goes on here but what does is motivated by one thing and one thing only: *pelota*. Many 'sons of Markina' have achieved star status in the sport, and the *frontón* is proudly dubbed the 'university of *pelota*'. As well as the more common *pelota a mano*, played with bare hands, there are regular games of *cesta punta*, in which a long wicker scoop is worn like a glove, adding some serious velocity to the game. Games are usually on a Sunday evening, but it's worth ringing the tourist office for details, or checking the website, www.euskalpilota.com – go to the 'Cartelera' section.

The hexagonal chapel of **San Miguel de Arretxmago** is a 10-minute stroll from the plaza on the other side of the small river. The building itself is unremarkable but inside, surprisingly, are three enormous rocks, naturally balanced, with an altar to the saint underneath that far predates the building. According to local tradition, St Michael buried the devil here; a lingering odour of brimstone would tend to confirm this. This is the place to be at midnight on 29 September, when the village gathers to perform two traditional dances, the *aurresku*, and the *mahai gaineko*. There's a summer **tourist office** in a palace across the iron footbridge over the river.

Lekeitio → *For listings, see pages 87-90.*

Along the Basque coastline, Lekeitio stands out as one of the best places to visit and stay. Its fully functioning fishing harbour is full of cheerfully painted boats, and the tall old houses seem to be jostling and squeezing each other for a front-row seat. Once a favourite of holidaying royalty, the town is lively at weekends and in summer, when it's a popular destination for Bilbao and San Sebastián families. There are two **beaches** – the one a bit further from town, across the bridge, is better. Both look across to the pretty rocky islet of the **Isla de San Nicolás** in the middle of the bay, covered in trees and home only to goats. The countryside around Lekeitio is beautiful, with rolling hills and jagged cliffs. The emerald green colour unfortunately doesn't come for nothing though – the town gets its fair share of rainy days.

The narrow streets backing the harbour conceal a few well-preserved medieval buildings, while the harbour itself is lined with bars. The **Iglesia de Santa María de la Asunción** is worth a visit. Lauded as one of the best examples of Basque Gothic architecture, it seems to change colour completely from dull grey to warm orange depending on the light. The *retablo* is an ornate piece of Flemish work, while the exterior has extravagant flying buttresses. The helpful **tourist information office** ① *C Independencia s/n, T946 844 017, turismo@learjai.com, Mon-Tue and Thu-Sat 1030-1330, 1600-1900, Sun 1030-1430; summer daily 1000-1400, 1600-2000*, has a good range of information.

Elantxobe

If tiny fishing villages are your thing, Elantxobe, west of Lekeitio, might be worth adding to your itinerary. With amazingly steep and narrow streets leading down to a small harbour, it seems a forgotten place, tucked away at the bottom of a sheer escarpment. It's authentic without being overly picturesque. There's now a road that winds around the hill down to the port, but the bus still gets spun around on a turntable in the tiny square up above. There are a few places to try the catch of the day, and a *hostal*. **Bizkaibus** A3513 between Bilbao and Lekeitio stops here. It leaves Bilbao every two hours from Calle Hurtado Amezaga by Abando train station.

Beyond Elantxobe, the coast is broken by the **Urdaibai estuary**, home to many waterbirds. The good beach of **Laia** looks across at the surfing village of **Mundaka**, but the road heads a fair way inland, crossing the river at the area's main town, Gernika.

Gernika/Guernica → *For listings, see pages 87-90.*

A name that weighs on the tongue, heavy with blood and atrocity, is Gernika, but this thriving town and symbol of Basque pride and nationalism has moved on from its tragic past, and provides the visitor with a great opportunity to experience Basque culture.

Today, Gernika is anything but a sombre memorial to the devastation it suffered (see box, page 78). While it understandably lacks much of its original architecture, it's a happy and friendly place that merits a visit. The Monday morning market is still very much in business and entertaining to check out. The **Casa de Juntas** ① *1000-1400, 1600-1800 (1900 in summer), free*, symbolically placed next to the famous oak tree, is once again the seat of the Vizcayan parliament. The highlight of the building itself is the room with a massive stained-glass roof depicting the oak tree. The tree itself is outside by the porch, while part of the trunk of an older one is enshrined in a slightly silly little pavilion. Behind the building is the **Parque de los Pueblos de Europa** ① *1000-1900 (2100 summer)*, which contains sculptures by Henry Moore and Eduardo Chillida. Both recall the devastated buildings of the town and are dedicated to peace.

Museo de la Paz

ⓘ *Plaza Foru 1, T946 270 213, www.museodelapaz.org. Tue-Sat 1000-1400, 1600-1900 (summer 1000-2000), Sun 1000-1400, €4.*

Gernika's showpiece, the Museo de la Paz (Museum of Peace), is an excellent and moving museum. It focuses on peace as a concept and as a goal to strive for, examines the Gernika bombing, then, crucially, the importance of reconciliation and an optimistic outlook. Two excellent audiovisual presentations are included; the staff cleverly put these in the right language as they monitor your progress through the museum. A visit to Gernika is highly recommended for this museum alone.

The **Euskal Herria Museoa** ⓘ *C Allendesalazar 5, T946 255 451, Tue-Sat 1000-1400, 1600-1900, Sun 1100-1430, 1600-2000, €3,* is housed in a strikingly beautiful 18th-century *palacio* and is the repository for a sizeable collection of artefacts relating to the history and ethnography of the Basque country.

Gernika has a **tourist office** ⓘ *Artekale 8, T946 255 892, turismo@gernika-lumo.net, Mon-Sat 1000-1400, 1600-1900, Sun 1000-1400; guided tours of the town leave here daily at 1100,* with English-speaking staff.

Around Gernika → *For listings, see pages 87-90.*

Gernika sits at the head of the estuary of the Río Oka, the **Urdaibai Reserve**, a varied area of tidal sandflats and riverbank ecology that is home to a huge amount of wildlife. UNESCO declared it a Biosphere Reserve in 1984. It's a great spot for birdwatching, but mammals such as the badger, marten and wild boar are also present. The **park headquarters** ⓘ *T946 257 125,* are on the edge of the town centre of Gernika in the Palacio de Udetxea on the far side of the Parque de los Pueblos. Vistas of the estuary can be had from either side of the estuary, but to really appreciate the area, you might be better off taking a tour.

Cueva de Santimamiñe

ⓘ *Tours cost €5 and are limited to 20 people on a first-come, first-served basis so should be booked ahead by phone T944 651 657, or email santimamine@bizkaia.net. They run Tue-Sun at 1000, 1030, 1200, 1230, 1500, 1530, 1700, and 1730. The visit lasts about 90 mins.*

The cave of Santimamiñe was an elegant and spacious home for thousands of generations of prehistoric folk, who decorated it with an important series of paintings depicting bison, among other animals. Apart from the entrance chamber, the cave is now closed to the public to protect the paintings and allow ongoing archaeological investigation, but it's still worth booking a guided visit. Starting with a stroll through the holm-oak hillside, you then visit the cave entrance and end up in an interpretation centre where you embark on a virtual visit of the entire cave while wearing 3D specs. Apart from the paintings, you see the eerily beautiful rock formations. The bus from Gernika to Lekeitio (approximately every two hours) can drop you at the turn-off just before the town of Kortezubi. From there it's a half-hour walk.

Bosque Pintado de Oma

ⓘ *Free.*

Near the caves is an unusual artwork: the Bosque Pintado de Oma. In a peaceful pine forest on a ridge, artist Agustín Ibarrola has painted eyes, people and geometric figures on the tree trunks in bright, bold colours. Some of the trees combine to form larger pictures – these can be difficult to make out, and it doesn't help that most of the display panels have been erased. Overall, it's a tranquil place with the wind whispering through the pines,

The bombing of Gernika

During the Spanish Civil War, in one of the most despicable planned acts of modern warfare there has ever been, 59 German and Italian planes destroyed the town in a bombardment that lasted three gruelling hours. It was 26 April, 1937, and market day in Gernika, thousands of villagers from the surrounding area were in the town, which had no air defences to call on. Three days earlier a similar bombardment had killed over 250 in the town of Durango, but the toll here was worse. Splinter and incendiary bombs were used for maximum impact, and fighters strafed fleeing people with machine guns. The attack resulted in about 1650 deaths.

Franco, the head of the Nationalist forces, simply denied the event had occurred; he claimed that any damage had been caused by Basque propagandists. In 1999 Germany formally apologized for the event, making the Spanish conspicuous by their silence. Apart from a general wish to terrorize and subdue the Basque population, who were resisting the Nationalist advance on Bilbao, Gernika's symbolic value was important. For many centuries Basque assemblies had met here under an oak tree – this was common to many Vizcayan towns but the Gernika meetings became dominant. They were attended by the monarch or a representative, who would swear to respect Basque rights and laws – the *fueros*. Thus the town became a powerful symbol of Basque liberty and nationhood. The first modern Basque government, a product of the Civil War, was sworn in under the oak only six months before the bombing.

One of the most famous results of the bombing was Picasso's painting, named after the town. He had been commissioned by the Republican government to paint a mural for the upcoming World Fair, and this was the result. It currently sits in the *Reina Sofía* gallery in Madrid although constant Basque lobbying may yet bring it to Bilbao. A ceramic copy has been made on a wall on Calle Allende Salazar in Gernika itself. Picasso commented on his painting: "By means of it, I express my abhorrence of the race that sunk Spain in an ocean of pain and death".

and there's a strangely primal quality about the work. It's hard not to feel that more could have been made of the original concept though. A dirt road climbs 3 km to the wood from opposite the **Lezika** restaurant next to the Santimamiñe caves. The forest is accessible by car, but it's a pleasant walk. If on foot, it's worth returning another way. Take the path down the hill at the other end of the Bosque from the entrance. After crossing a couple of fields, you'll find yourself in the tiny hamlet of **Oma**, with attractive Basque farmhouses. Turning left along the road will lead you back to the caves.

Mundaka and Bermeo → For listings, see pages 87-90. Colour map 3, B2.

From Gernika, following the west bank of the estuary takes you back to the coast. A brisk half-hour's walk is all that separates the fishing towns of Bermeo and Mundaka, but they couldn't be more different. Mundaka is petite and slightly upmarket as visitors come to admire its beautiful harbour. Bermeo puts it in the shade in fishing terms: as one of the most important ports on this coast some of its boats seem bigger than Mundaka's harbour. There's a good atmosphere though, and an attractive old town.

Cod, whales and America

In former times whales were a common species off the northern coast of Spain. The Basques were among the first to hunt the giant mammals, which they were doing as far back as the seventh century. It became a major enterprise and, as the whales grew scarcer, they had to go further afield, venturing far into the North Atlantic. It's a good bet they reached America in the 14th century at the latest, signing the native Americans' visitors book under the Vikings and the shadowy, debatable scrawl of St Brendan.

The whaling expeditions provisioned themselves by fishing and preserving cod during the trip. The folk back home got a taste for this *bacalao*, and they still love it, to the bemusement of many tourists. Meanwhile, Elkano added to the Basques' seafaring CV by becoming the first man to circumnavigate the globe, after the expedition leader, Magellan, was killed in the Philippines. Basque whalers established many settlements along the coast of Labrador during the 16th century and, later, Basques left their homes in droves for the promise of the New World; Basque culture has been significant in the development of the USA, particularly in some of the western states, as well as in Argentina and Chile.

Mundaka

While Mundaka still has its small fishing fleet, it's better known as a surfing village. It's a Mecca of the global surf community, with a magnificent left-break (a wave that breaks from right to left, looking towards the beach). When the wind blows and the big waves roll in, a good surfer can jump in off the rocks by Mundaka harbour and ride a wave right across the estuary mouth to Laida beach, a couple of kilometres away. Even if catching waves isn't your thing, Mundaka is still well worth visiting, with a beautiful bonsai harbour and relaxed ambience. The village is a small maze of winding streets and an oversized church. There are some good places to stay or camp, and it's within striking distance of several highlights of the Basque coast. In summer, boats run across to **Laida beach**, which is the best in the area. It's almost worth the trip merely to taste the *tigres* at the small bar on the estuary. There's a small **tourist office** ① *Mon, Wed, Fri 1130-1430, longer hours in summer*, near Mundaka's harbour. The town's surf shop, www.mundakasurfshop.com, is the place to go for equipment and advice.

Bermeo

Bermeo is a bigger and more typical Basque fishing town with a more self-sufficient feel. One of the whaling towns that more or less pioneered the activity on this coast, Bermeo has a proud maritime history documented in its museum. The ships for Columbus's second voyage were built and largely crewed from here. There's much more action in the fishing harbour here than in peaceful Mundaka.

The old town is worth a visit. There's a cobbled square across which the church and the Ayuntamiento vie for power; the latter has a sundial on its face. There's a small chunk of the old town wall preserved, with a symbolic footprint of John the Baptist, who is said to have made modern triple jumpers weep by leaping from here to the sanctuary of Gaztelugatxe in three steps. The **Museo del Pescador** ① *Plaza Torrontero 1, T946 881 171, Tue-Sat 1000-1400, 1600-1900, Sun 1000-1415, €3*, is set in a 15th-century tower and is devoted to the Basque fishing industry. The tourist office is opposite the station.

If you want to get out on the water, **Hegaluze** ① *T666 791 021, www.hegaluze.com*, runs coastal trips, whale- and dolphin-watching excursions, and cruises in the Urdaibai estuary in a small covered boat.

Santuario de San Juan de Gaztelugatxe and around
West of Bermeo, some 6 km from town, is the spectacular sanctuary of San Juan de Gaztelugatxe. In the early 11th century, Sancho the Great, King of Navarra, was in Aquitaine, in France, when a surprising gift was presented to the local church hierarchy: the head of John the Baptist, which had mysteriously turned up a short while before. As a result, the cult of the Baptist received an understandable boost and many monasteries and sanctuaries were built in his name, including several in northeastern Spain, with the express encouragement of the impressed Sancho.

San Juan de Gaztelugatxe is one of these (although the church dates from much later). A rocky island frequently rendered impressively bleak by the coastal squalls, is connected by a bridge to the mainland, from where it's 231 steps to the top. Apart from the view, there's not a great deal to see, but the setting is spectacular. The island is a pilgrimage spot, particularly for the feast of St John on 24 June, and also on 31 July. To get there from Bermeo, take a bus (about every two hours) along the coast road towards Bakio; you can get off opposite the sanctuary. While you're here, have lunch at the Eneperi, overlooking the sanctuary with a superb terrace, cheap lunches and *pintxos* in the bar, an excellent, more upmarket, restaurant, and even a small museum.

Vizcayan Coast listings

For Sleeping and Eating price codes and other relevant information, see pages 12-19.

☺ Sleeping

Ondarroa *p75*
€ Patxi, Arta Bide 21, T609 986 446. On the sloping street heading down into the town when coming from the west, this is an exceedingly good-value *pensión* with comfortable rooms and a shared bathroom.

Markina Xemein *p75*
€€-€ Intxauspe, Barrio Atxondo 10, T652 770 889, www.intxauspe.com. Just north of the centre of Markina, this beautifully restored stone farmhouse is a *casa rural* that has a caring owner and 5 pretty, comfortable rooms, ideal for a relaxing stay in this corner of rural Vizcaya.

Lekeitio *p76*
€€€ Hotel Palacio Oxangoiti, Gamarra Kalea 2, T944 650 555, www.oxangoiti.net.

This loving new conversion of a 17th-century palace in the heart of town will win you over with its friendly welcome and elegant old-style decor. It's an intimate place with just 7 rooms (the bathrooms are gleamingly modern), so you'll need to book ahead.
€€ Hotel Zubieta, Portal de Atea, T946 843 030, www.hotelzubieta.com. A superbly converted coachhouse in the grounds of a *palacio*. With surprisingly low prices, this is one of the best places to stay, with friendly management, a lively bar, and cosy rooms with sloping wooden ceilings. Light sleepers, however, will enjoy it more at weekends, for the woodyard next door can be noisy on weekday mornings. Recommended. Also has reasonably priced apartments for 2-4.
€€ Emperatriz Zita/Aisia Lekeitio, Santa Elena Etorbidea s/n, T946 842 655, www.aisiahoteles.com. This slightly odd-looking hotel was built on the site of a palace where Empress Zita had lived in the 1920s. Married to the last Austro-Hungarian emperor, who

unluckily acceded to the throne in a losing position in World War 1; she was left with 8 children when he died of pneumonia on Madeira in 1922. The hotel is furnished in fading but appropriately elegant style and is also a thalassotherapy (sea water) health centre. It was badly in need of a refit when we last passed by, so until that happens, look elsewhere.

€€ Piñupe Hotela, Av Pascual Abaroa 10, T946 842 984. The cheapest place in town and a sound choice. The rooms have en suite, phone and TV and are far more comfortable than the bar downstairs indicates.

Elantxobe *p76*

€€-€ Elantxobe Ostatua, Aita Arriandiaga 5, T946 276 344. This spruce little place has just 4 rooms, with small modern bathrooms and great views down over the fishing harbour.

Gernika *p76*

€€ Hotel Katxi, Morga/Andra Mari s/n, T946 270 740, www.katxi.com. A few kilometres west of Gernika in the hamlet of Morga is this excellent rural hotel. The rooms, some much larger than others, are extremely comfortable, and there's a friendly lounge area. It's a great place to get away from things, with a warm atmosphere, and plenty of opportunity for relaxing on the terrace or in the garden. The owners run a good *asador* next door.

€€ Hotel Gernika, C Carlos Gangoiti 17, T946 250 350, www.hotel-gernika.com. Gernika's best hotel is nothing exceptional, situated on the main road at the edge of town. But it's had a recent facelift, and the comfortable rooms are backed up by facilities including a café, and helpful service.

€€-€ Pensión Akelarre, C Barrenkale 5, T946 270 197, www.hotelakelarre.com. This enjoyable place has funky little rooms with TV and varnished floorboards. There's a terrace to take some sun and it's in the heart of the pedestrian area. There's free Wi-Fi access.

There are discounts if you stay more than 1 night, and it's significantly cheaper off-season. If there's nobody there, you can access and pay via a computer terminal. Recommended.
€ Hotel Boliña, C Barrenkale 3, T946 250 300, www.hotelbolina.net. In the centre of Gernika, this hotel has some good-value doubles with TV and telephone. It's well run and makes a good choice, although it can be stuffy in the height of summer.

€ Pensión Madariaga, C Industria 10, T946 256 035. Very attractively furnished rooms with TV, bathroom and heating. Good value.

Mundaka *p79*

Accommodation in Mundaka isn't cheap.
€€€ Hotel Atalaya, C Itxaropen 1, T946 177 000, www.hotelatalaya.es. The classier of the town's options, recently refurbished and with a summery feel to its rooms and café. Garden and parking adjoin the stately building. Very nice breakfasts (not included) and excellent service round out the package.

€€ Hotel El Puerto, Portu Kalea 1, T946 876 725, www.hotelelpuerto.com. The best value of Mundaka's 3 hotels, set right by the tiny fishing harbour. Delightful rooms, very cosy and some overlooking the harbour (worth paying the few extra euro). The bar below is one of Mundaka's best but noise can carry to the rooms above it. Free Wi-Fi. Recommended.

€€ Hotel Mundaka, C Florentino Larrinaga 9, T946 876 700, www.hotelmundaka. com. This well-cared for hotel offers rather pleasant rooms just back from the water, with plenty of space and comfortable beds. There's also a garden and café-bar as well as internet access and Wi-Fi.

Camping

Portuondo, 1 km out of Mundaka on the road to Gernika, T946 877 701, www. campingportuondo.com. Sardined during the summer months, this is a well-equipped campsite with a swimming pool, cafés and laundry. There are several bungalows (a week minimum stay in high summer) that sleep up to 4, but are not significantly cheaper than the hotels in town if you're only 2. They do come with kitchen, fridge, and television though.

Bermeo p79

€€ Hostal Torre Ercilla, C Talaranzko 14, T946 187 598, barrota@piramidal.com.
A lovely place to stay in Bermeo's old town, between the museum and church. Rooms are designed for relaxation, with small balconies, reading nooks and soft carpet. There's also a lounge, terrace, chessboard and BBQ among other comforts. Recommended.

🍴 Eating

Ondarroa p75

¶¶ Eretegia Joxe Manuel, C Sabino Arana 23, T946 830 104. Although it does a range of other appetizing dishes, the big charcoal grill outside this restaurant caters to carnivores with large appetites. Forget quarter-pounders; here the steaks approach the kilogram mark and are very juicy and tasty. Go for the *buey* (ox) for extra flavour.
¶¶ Sutargi, Nasa Kalea 11, T946 832 258.
A popular bar with an excellent restaurant upstairs serving traditional Basque seafood specialities. Difficult to get a table at weekends.

Lekeitio p76

Despite the busy summer scene, there are lots of fairly traditional places to eat and drink.
¶¶ Kaia, Txatxo kaia 5, T946 840 284. One of the many harbourside restaurants and bars, this serves excellent grilled fresh fish. There's a daily lunch *menú* for €12 too.
¶¶ Zapiraín, C Igualdegi 3, T946 840 255.
This cosy family-run spot is something of a Lekeitio classic and excels itself with warm personal service and fantastic fresh fish.

Gernika p76

¶¶ Arrien, C Eriabarrena 1, T946 258 551.
Overlooking the flowery Jardines de El Ferial,

this terraced restaurant/bar has a good *menú del día* for €9 and various other set meals from €10 as well as à la carte selections.
¶ Foruria, C Industria 10, T946 251 020.
A good option for a cheapish meal, with a selection of hot dishes around the €9 mark as well as a wide selection of *jamón*, *chorizo* and cheese for cold platters. There are several other options on this street.

Around Gernika p77

¶¶ Lezika, Cuevas de Santimamiñe, Kortezubi, T946 252 975. The whole of Vizcaya seems to descend on the beer garden here at weekends with kids and dogs in tow; the restaurant is worthwhile as well and better value than the meagre *raciones* on offer at the bar.

Mundaka p79

¶¶ Asador Bodegón, Kepa Deuna 1, T946 876 353. Mundaka's best restaurant, despite a slight air of 'we know what you want to eat'. Meat and especially fresh fish are grilled to perfection over the coals. Try the home-made *patxarán*, a liqueur made from sloe berries. Upstairs is **Casino**, a traditional members' club that's also a high-quality restaurant with a very old-fashioned feel and great views from the gallery. Fish is the thing to try here.

🍸 Bars and clubs

Ondarroa p75

Ondarroa's nightlife scene revolves around the main streets of the old centre. **Nasa Kalea** is well-stocked with bars, many of which are temples to Basque rock, which is heavily identified with the Independence movement.
Music school, corner of Iñaki Deunaren and Sabino Arana (Arana'tar Sabin). Often has live Basque alternative rock on Fri or Sat nights – it's usually free.

Lekeitio p76

Hotel Zubieta, Portal de Atea, T946 843 030.
The lively café bar in this beautifully restored

coachhouse is an excellent spot for a chat and a beverage in uplifting surroundings.
Talako Bar, above the fisherman's cooperative on the harbour, is a great spot for one of Lekeitio's rainy days, with a pool table, board games and a 180° view of the harbour, town and beaches.
Txalupa, Txatxo kaia 7. While Lekeitio isn't as out-and-out Basque as Ondarroa, this bar on the harbourside keeps the Basque rock pumping, and does a range of simple snacks.

___

Gernika *p76*
Arrana, C Juan Calzada 6. A vibrant Basque bar with a lively young crowd spilling outside at weekends.
Metropol, corner of C Unamuno and Iparragirre. A cavernous and comradely bar, open later than anywhere else.

⊛ Festivals and events

Lekeitio *p76*
5 Sep Fiesta de San Antolín. In a land of strange festivals, this is one of the strangest. It involves a long rope, a few rowing boats, plenty of able-bodied young folk and a goose. Thankfully these days the goose is already dead. The hapless bird is tied in the middle of the rope, which is stretched across the harbour and held at both ends. Competitors take turns from rowing boats to grab the goose's head (which has been liberally greased up) under their arm. The rope is then tightened, lifting the grabber high into the air, and then slackened,

dunking them in the water. This is repeated until either the goose's head comes off, or the person falls off, when it's time for the next boat's turn.

⊖ Transport

Ondarroa *p75*
Ondarroa is served by Bizkaibus from **Bilbao** bus station (hourly) via **Markina** and Pesa from **San Sebastián** bus station (50 mins), 4 times a day (twice at weekends).

___

Lekeitio *p76*
Bizkaibus hourly from the bus station in **Bilbao** (30 mins), Pesa 4 a day from the bus station in **San Sebastián** (2 at weekends, 1 hr 25 mins).

___

Gernika *p76*
There are hourly trains to Gernika from **Bilbao**'s Atxuri station, and buses ½ hourly (hourly at weekends) from C Hurtado de Amezaga next to Abando station (30 mins).

___

Mundaka and Bermeo *p78*
Hourly trains to both towns from **Bilbao**'s Atxuri station, and ½-hourly buses from C Hurtado de Amezaga next to Abando station.

⊙ Directory

Lekeitio *p76*
Internet Ziber Jaure, C Agirre Solarte 17, €2 per hr.

Vitoria/Gasteiz

Vitoria is the quiet achiever of the trio of Basque cities. A comparatively peaceful town, it comes as a surprise to many visitors to discover that it's actually the capital of the semi-autonomous Basque region. A thoughtful place, it combines an attractive old town with an Ensanche (expansion) designed to provide plenty of green spaces for its hard-working inhabitants. While it lacks the big-city vitality of Bilbao or the languid beauty of San Sebastián it's a satisfying city much-loved by most who visit it. Perhaps because it's the political centre of the region, the young are very vocally Basque, and the city feels energized as a result. An ambitious urban improvement plan has brought escalators to the old town, a tram service, and is creating a flash new train/bus station to the north of the centre. ▸ *For listings, see pages 88-91.*

Ins and outs → *Phone code: 945. Population: 239,361. Altitude: 512 m.*

Getting there There are frequent bus connections with Bilbao and other Basque destinations. Vitoria's **RENFE** station has better connections with the rest of Spain than does Bilbao. ▸ *See Transport, page 91.*

Getting around Vitoria is a good two-wheel city with more cycle ways and green spots than in busier Bilbao. There's a new tram line, but Vitoria is easily walkable with Calle Dato the focus of the evening paseo.

Tourist information Vitoria's **tourist office** ⓘ *Plaza General Loma 1, T945 161 598, turismo@vitoria-gasteiz.org, summer daily 0930-1930, winter Mon-Sat 1000-1900, Sun 1100-1400,* is in the centre of things.

Background

Vitoria's shield-shaped old town sits on the high ground that perhaps gave the city its name (*beturia* is an Euskara word for hill). After being a Basque settlement first, then a Roman one, Vitoria was abandoned until it was refounded and fortified by the kings of Navarra in the 12th and 13th centuries. An obscure Castilian town for much of its history, Vitoria featured in the Peninsular War, when, on midsummer's day in 1813, Napoleon's forces were routed by the Allied troops and fled in ragged fashion towards home, abandoning their baggage train containing millions of francs, which was gleefully looted. "The battle was to the French", commented a British officer sagely, "like salt on a leech's tail". Vitoria has thrived since being named capital of the semi-autonomous Basque region, and has a genteel, comfortable air, enlivened by an active student population.

Casco Medieval

Calle Cuchillería and Calle Chiquita

Calle Cuchillería, and its continuation, Calle Chiquita, is the liveliest part of the old town, with several impressive old mansions, a couple of museums, dozens of bars, and plenty of pro-Basque political attitude. Indeed, there's an interesting contrast in the atmosphere of the new and old towns; whereas the former feels very Spanish and quite staid, the preserve of middle-aged strollers, the old streets hum with young Basque energy. Like several in the Casco Medieval, this street is named after the craftspeople who used to have shops here; in this case knife makers. Walking along this street and those nearby you can see a number of old inscriptions and coats of arms carved on buildings.

Housed in a beautiful fortified medieval house on Cuchillería with a sleek modern extension out the back **Bibat** ① *Tue-Fri 1000-1400, 1600-1830, Sat 1000-1400, Sun 1100-1400, free*, contains two museums. The unusual Fournier collection is devoted to the playing card, of which it holds over 10,000 packs. Diamonds are forever, but you won't see many here: the cards are mostly Spanish decks, with swords, cups, coins and staves the suits. Here also is the archaeology museum. The province has been well occupied over history, and the smallish collection covers many periods, from prehistoric through Roman and medieval. Arguably the most impressive of the objects on display is the *Knight's Stele*, a tombstone carved with a horseman dating from the Roman era.

The corner of the old town at the end of Calle Chiquita is one of Vitoria's most picturesque. The **Casa del Portalón**, now a restaurant, is a lovely old timbered building from the late 15th century. It used to be an inn and a staging post for messengers. Across from it is the **Torre de los Anda**, which defended one of the entrances in the city wall. Opposite these is the 16th-century house of the Gobeo family.

Opposite here is the current entrance to the older of Vitoria's two cathedrals, the **Catedral de Santa María** ① *tours daily 1100-1400, 1700-2000, €3 per person, pre-book on T945 255 135 or www.catedral vitoria.com*. There's an ongoing restoration project, scheduled to last until 2012. It's currently 'open for renovation'; while normal visits have been suspended, you can take a fascinating guided tour of the restoration works. Depending on the progress, you may be able to walk on gangways high above the nave, admiring the vaulting from close up, or see the delicate retrieval of crumbling stonework.

Above the busy square of **Plaza de la Virgen Blanca**, the church of **San Miguel** stands like one of a series of chess pieces guarding the entrance to the Casco Medieval. Two gaping arches mark the portal, which is superbly carved. A niche here holds the city's patron saint, the Virgen Blanca, a coloured late-Gothic figure. On the saint's day, 5 August, a group of townspeople carry the figure of Celedón (a stylized farmer) from the top of the graceful belltower down to the square.

Los Arquillos

Running off the same square, this slightly strange series of dwellings and covered colonnades was designed in the early 19th century as a means of more effectively linking the high Casco Medieval with the newer town below, and to avoid the risk of the collapse of the southern part of the hill. It leads up to the attractive small **Plaza del Machete**, where incoming city chancellors used to swear an oath of allegiance over a copy of the Fueros (city statutes) and a machete, in this case a military cutlass.

Also off Plaza de la Virgen Blanca, the picture-postcard **Plaza de España** (Basques prefer to call it **Plaza Nueva**) was designed by the same man, Olaguíbel, who thought up

Vitoria/Gasteiz

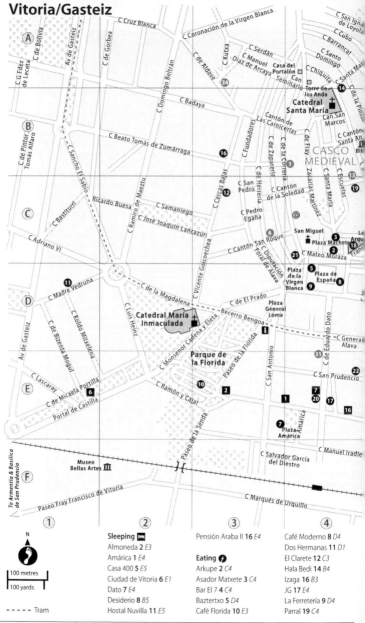

Sleeping 🛏
Almoneda 2 *E3*
Amárica 1 *E4*
Casa 400 5 *E5*
Ciudad de Vitoria 6 *E1*
Dato 7 *E4*
Desiderio 8 *B5*
Hostal Nuvilla 11 *E5*
Pensión Araba II 16 *E4*

Eating 🍴
Arkupe 2 *C4*
Asador Matxete 3 *C4*
Bar El 7 4 *C4*
Baztertxo 5 *D4*
Café Florida 10 *E3*

Café Moderno 8 *D4*
Dos Hermanas 11 *D1*
El Clarete 12 *C3*
Hala Bedi 14 *B4*
Izaga 16 *B3*
JG 17 *E4*
La Ferretería 9 *D4*
Parral 19 *C4*

100 metres
100 yards

- - - - - Tram

the Arquillos. It's a beautiful colonnaded square busy with playing children and parents chatting over coffee, housing the town hall and several bars with terraces that are perfect for the morning or afternoon sun.

New Town

Vitoria's new town isn't going to blow anyone's mind with a cavalcade of Gaudí-esque buildings or wild street parties, but it is a very satisfying place: a planned mixture of attractive streets and plenty of parkland. It's got the highest amount of greenery per citizen of any city in Spain and it's no surprise that it's been voted one of the best places to live in the coutry. With the innovative Artium adding a touch of innovation, the mantle of Basque capital seems to sit ever easier on Vitoria's shoulders.

Artium

ⓘ C Francia 24, T945 209 020, www.artium. org, Tue-Thu 1100-1400, 1700-2000, Fri-Sun 1100-1400, 1600-2100, entry by donation.
Artium is Vitoria's answer to Bilbao's Guggenheim and San Sebastián's Kursaal. It's an exciting project that features some excellent contemporary artwork, mostly in the form of temporary exhibitions, some of which incorporate some of the older buildings in Vitoria's Casco Medieval. Shiny and white, your attention is grabbed immediately by the building's confident angles and Javier Pérez's *Un pedazo de cielo cristalizado* (A piece of sky made glass), a large hanging-glass sculpture in the atrium. The galleries are accessed down the stairs. The website has details in English about what's on at any given time; the exhibitions are usually in place for many months. There's also a good little café.

Catedral de María Inmaculada

There's no missing the new cathedral, María Inmaculada, constructed in the 20th century in neo-Gothic style; its bulk looms

C de Hortaleza

C del Monseñor Estenaga

C de Pedro Orbea

C Sierras Alavesas

San Ildefonso   C de Arana

C de la Esperanza

Colegio de San Prudencio   Artium   C de Logroño

C Prudencio María Verástegui

El Torno   Abrevadero   C José de Mardones

C Nueva Fuera   C de la Libertad   Los Herran

C Nueva Dentro   C Francia   Pje Santiago

C San   Av de Santiago
ancisco   C Portal del Rey

CDM Álava

C de Olaguíbel   C Don Juan

C de Postas

C de La Paz

de la Independencia   C Doce de Octubre

C Fueros   C Jesús Guridi   C de Pío XII

Ortiz de Zárate   C Canciller Ayala

C de la Florida   C Rioja   Juan XXIII

Isaac Albéniz

⑤   ⑥

attractively over this part of the town. Built in medieval style, it now houses the **Museo Diocesano de Arte Sacro** ① *Tue-Fri 1000-1400, 1600-1830, Sat 1000-1400, Sun 1100-1400, free.*

Parque de la Florida

This gorgeous park is an excellent retreat right in the heart of Vitoria. Cool and shady, it has a number of exotic trees and plants and a couple of peaceful cafés. You can watch old men in berets playing *bolas* (boules), and there's an old bandstand with Sunday concerts, guarded by statues of four ancient kings. If you see anyone taking life a little too seriously, they're more than likely politicians – the Basque Parliament stands in a corner of the park.

Basílica de San Prudencio

① *Mon-Fri 1000-1400, Sat 1000-1400, 1600-2100, Sun 1000-1200, 1600-2100, guided visit €3.*
It's well worth the half-hour walk or the bus ride to see this church in the village of **Armentia**, now subsumed into Vitoria's outskirts. The village is supposedly the birthplace of San Prudencio, the patron saint of Alava Province, and the church was erected in his honour. It was rebuilt in the 18th century, but still has some excellent features from its Romanesque youth, such as a harmonious round apse and the carvings above the doors, one of Christ and the apostles, the other of the Lamb and John the Baptist. At time of writing, it was being renovated, and access to most of the building was by guided tour run by archaeologists who have exposed Romanesque foundations and an adjoining cemetery.

To reach Armentia on foot, continue past the Museo de Bellas Artes on Paseo Fray Francisco de Vitoria, then turn left down Paseo de Cervantes when you reach the modern chapel of **La Sagrada Familia**. The basilica is at the end of this road. It's a pleasant walk; you can also get bus No 9, which runs every half an hour from the new cathedral to the basilica.

Vitoria/Gasteiz listings

For Sleeping and Eating price codes and other relevant information, see pages 12-19.

◎ Sleeping

Vitoria *p84, map p86*
€€€ Parador de Argómaniz, Carretera N1 Km 363, T945 293 200, www.parador.es. This parador is some 12 km east of Vitoria in a Renaissance palace. It's a tranquil place with some good views over the surrounding countryside. Napoleon slept here before the disastrous Battle of Vitoria.
€€€ Hotel Ciudad de Vitoria, Portal de Castilla 8, T945 141 100, www.hoteles-silken.com. A massive 4-star hotel situated at the edge of Vitoria's centre, where character starts to make way for 'lifestyle'. It's airy and pleasant, with good facilities, including a gym

and sauna. Chief attraction is its excellent weekend rate, when it's usually a €€.
€€ Hotel Almoneda, C Florida 7, T945 154 084, www.hotelalmoneda.com. Attractively situated a few paces from the lovely Parque de la Florida, this hotel has decent spacious rooms with a rustic touch. It's significantly cheaper at weekends. Breakfast included; you can even have it in bed if you ask nicely.
€€ Hotel América, C Florida 11, T945 130 506. Just around the corner from C Dato and close to the train station, this friendly hotel is very well placed. The rooms are good value, with TV and good bathroom, warm, and surprisingly quiet, considering it's a busy street.
€€ Hotel Dato, C Eduardo Dato 28, T945 147 230, www.hoteldato.com. This *pintxo*-zone cheap hotel is a treasury of art nouveau

and classic statues, mirrors and general plushness, in a comfortable rather than stuffy way. Its rooms are exceptional value too; all are pretty, with excellent facilities, and some have balconies or miradors (enclosed balconies). Free Wi-Fi. Recommended.

€€ Hotel Desiderio, C Colegio San Prudencio 2, T945 251 700, www.hoteldesiderio.es. This is a welcoming hotel with unremarkable but comfy rooms with bathroom just on the edge of the Casco Medieval. It's quiet and unassuming and offers very good value. They have cheaper *hostal* rooms across the road.

€ Pensión Araba II, C Florida 25, T945 232 588, www.pensionaraba.com. This elegant home makes an excellent base in central Vitoria. A variety of spotless, comfortable rooms with or without bathroom and a genuinely friendly welcome make it a budget star. Parking spaces available (€6).

€ Casa 400, C Florida 46, T945 233 887, p.gandiaga@telefonica.net. This renovated *pensión* makes a sound central base. Spacious rooms have comfortable beds, decent bathrooms and electronic locks; the friendly owner will show you the ropes then leave you to your own devices. There's free Wi-Fi and it's handy for the train station.

€ Hostal Nuvilla, C Fueros 29, T945 259 151. Centrally located *pensión* with small rooms with washbasin. It's friendly and cheap

🍴 Eating

Vitoria *p84, map p86*
In the old town, C Cuchillería is a long row of simple Basque taverns; smarter places dot the new town, particularly around C Eduardo Dato.

🍴🍴🍴 Arkupe, C Mateo Moraza 13, T945 230 080, www.restaurantearkupe.com. On the edge of the old town, this quality restaurant turns out imaginative dishes that are typically combinations of various quality northern Spanish products. Try the juicy *carrilleras* stewed in local Rioja, the range of gourmet salads, or, on Thu, a traditional *cocido* stew.

🍴🍴🍴 Dos Hermanas, C Madre Vedruna 10, T945 132 934, www.restaurantedoshermanas.com. One of Vitoria's oldest restaurants, this place manages to combine tradition and modernity, with an assured gourmet touch and personable service. There's a variety of set menus as well as some à la carte options.

🍴🍴 El Clarete, C Cercas Bajas 18, T945 263 874, www.elclareterestaurante.com. Comfortably contemporary in style, this enthusiastically run restaurant offers confidently prepared modern Spanish cuisine with an experimental flair. Portions, while not huge, are beautifully presented and taste fabulous: try the slow-roasted lamb or anything with their home-made foie.

🍴🍴 Asador Matxete, Plaza Machete 4, T945 131 821, www.matxete.com. This stylish, friendly restaurant is harmoniously inserted into this pretty plaza above Los Arquillos. The vaulted dining area is atmospheric, and dishes such as quail salad back up the excellent charcoal-grilled meat, though service is a little patchy. There's also a quality downstairs tapas bar and pleasant terrace to enjoy a drink in this peaceful square.

🍴🍴 Baztertxo, Plaza de España 14, T945 157 400. A fine bar with some great wines by the glass and top-notch *jamón* and other gourmet snacks. Although service can be beneath the dignity of the staff, it's still a good choice, with a terrace on the square.

🍴🍴 Izaga, Tomás de Zumárraga 2, T945 138 200, www.restauranteizaga.com. Excellent dining at this fairly formal restaurant in a smart stone building. The focus is on seafood – try the delicious Huelva prawns – but there are plenty of other specialities – such as duck's liver on stuffed pig's ear, and some sinful desserts. There's a *menú del día* on weekdays for €21.

🍴🍴 Toloño, Cuesta San Francisco 3, T945 233 336. One of the city's best *pintxo* bars, this smart spot on the hill leading up to the old town is a kidney-shaped space with an upbeat and welcoming feel. The tapas are great, especially the gourmet *pintxos* chalked up on the board. For around €3, take your pick from a range of exquisite hot delights; the *foie* is great if it's on. Recommended.

¶¶ Xixilu, Plaza Amárica 2, T945 230 068. On a small gardened square not far from the train station, this is a great place to eat. The sociable, intimate *comedor* at the back is filled with chunky wooden tables and stools; the food is quite smart, with delicate *sesos* (brains), and good house salad among a range of tempting dishes. Recommended.

¶ Bar El 7, C Cuchillería 7, T945 272 298. A Vitoria classic, this is an excellent bar at the head of the Casco Medieval's liveliest street. Its big range of *bocadillos* keeps students and all-comers happy. Order a half if you're not starving; they make 'em pretty large. They also do a very acceptable €11 *menú del día*.

¶ Hala Bedi, C Cuchillería 98, T945 260 411. A late-opening Basque bar with a cheerful atmosphere. It's very lively, and popular with the young and politically conscious. Out of a tiny kitchen come crêpes with a massive variety of sweet and savoury fillings, as well as sandwiches and other simple dishes.

¶ Parral, Cantón de San Francisco Javier 4. T945 276 833. This relaxed spot on a sloping street above C Cuchillería is a vegetarian restaurant by day and a mood bar by night, with regular live music. There's a salad buffet and a *menú del día* offering significant value.

¶ Restaurante JG, C Eduardo Dato 27, T945 231 132. Another excellent option for *pintxos* on this pedestrian street – the range of *croquetas* comes highly recommended. More substantial eating is also good value in the *comedor*.

¶ Restaurante Virgen Blanca, Plaza Virgen Blanca s/n, T945 286 199. Overlooking the picturesque Virgen Blanca square, this spacious spot features sturdy wooden tables and gnarled floorboards, as well as great outdoor tables perfect for contemplation of central Vitoria. Tasty *pintxos* are arrayed along the bar, and there's a lunch *menú* for €14.70.

¶ Saburdi, C Eduardo Dato 32, T945 147 016. There are some excellent *pintxo* bars in

Vitoria, and this is one of the classics, with a great range of delicious bites. It's warmly lit and welcoming, with several decent wines by the glass. Recommended.

¶ Taberna, C San Prudencio 21. Simple dynamics: long bar, tables in the sun, big screen showing sport or films, beer, wine and *pintxos*. It spills onto the street in a happy crowd in summer.

Cafés

Café Moderno, Plaza España 4. Sunseekers should head here in the afternoon – the terrace in the picture-postcard arched square is perfectly placed for maximum rays. The trendy bar does good *pintxos*, and the terrace gets very lively in the evenings as the square packs out with socializing Vitorians.

Café Florida, Parque de la Florida. One of Vitoria's best spots, with lots of tables among the trees of this peaceful park. Regular games of *bolas* take place nearby.

La Ferretería, Plaza de la Virgen Blanca s/n, T945 133 922. In the heart of Vitoria, this trendily lit former ironmongers is not to be sneered at if you're on the prowl for a morning coffee and croissant. If you grab a spot on its terrace in the early evening you can truly say you are sitting where it's all happening.

🎵 Bars and clubs

Vitoria *p84*, map *p86*

The old town tends to have boisterous, no-frills bars with a Basque atmosphere, while the new town has a more chic scene.

Bar Río, C Eduardo Dato 20, T945 230 067. A decent café with outdoor tables by day, and one of the last bars to shut at night, when it caters to a good-natured gay/straight crowd. They prepare mixed drinks with an unbelievably elaborate ritual. Original live music on Thu nights.

Café Iguana, Correría 94, T945 122 837. This spot has a great ambience for an after-dinner *copa* and a friendly mix of arty people. Plenty of tables and well-mixed drinks. One of Vitoria's best.

Cairo Stereo Club, C Aldabe 9. Great club with some excellent and innovative DJs and a mixed crowd. During the week they often show cult movies or hold theme parties.
El Bodegón de Gorbea, C Herrería 26. A classic. No-frills bar with rock music, cheap beer, and a bohemian bunch of friendly Basques chatting and drinking from early until very late. On the corner of Cantón San Roque.
Gora, Cantón de San Francisco Javier s/n. A modern, spacious place just off C Cuchillería. Green, light and peaceful.

⊛ Festivals and events

Vitoria *p84, map p86*
25 Jul Santiago's day is celebrated as the Día del Blusa, when colour-coordinated kids patrol the streets.
4-9 Aug Fiesta de la Virgen Blanca, the city's major knees-up, which is recommended.
Dec Advent. Vitoria is known for its spectacular life-sized Nativity scene (*Belén*), with over 200 figures.

⊙ Shopping

Vitoria *p84, map p86*
Segunda Mano, C Prudencio María Verástegui 14, T945 270 007. This is an amazing shop selling second-hand goods, which seems to have everything. From books to grand pianos, skis to tractors, and carriages to confessionals. You name it, it's likely to be there.

⊖ Transport

Vitoria *p84, map p86*
Air
Vitoria's airport (VIT) is 8 km northwest of town. The airport is served by **Iberia** affiliates from **Madrid** and **Barcelona**. A taxi from the centre will cost about €17.

Bus
Until the new bus station is built (this will be at tram stop: Intermodal), the bus station is on the eastern side of town. Buses to **Bilbao** run about every 30 mins with **Autobuses La Unión** (55 mins, €6). There are 7-8 buses a day to **San Sebastián** (1 hr 40 mins, €8), to **Madrid** (€25, 5 hrs), **Burgos** (€8, 1½ hrs), **Pamplona** (9-14 daily, €8, 1 hr 40 mins), as well as buses to **Logroño**, **Haro**, **Laguardia**, and **Salvatierra**.

Taxi
A taxi ride from Vitoria train station to the Basilica at Armentia costs about €6.

Train
The train station has regular connections with **Madrid**, **Zaragoza**, **Logroño**, **Barcelona**, **Burgos**, and other destinations.

Tram
Vitoria's smart new tram line crosses the city centre and costs €1.05 for a ride. It's not of great use to the visitor yet, but will be once the new bus station opens north of the town in a few years.

❶ Directory

Vitoria *p84, map p86*
Internet and telephone Locutorio Tito, C Correría 44, and **Meknasi**, C Fueros 7, have cheap internet and phone calls.

Alava Province

The province of Alava is something of a wilderness compared to the densely settled valleys of Vizcaya and Guipúzcoa. It's the place to come for unspoiled nature; there are some spots of great natural beauty and plenty of scope for hiking and other more specialized outdoor activities. The attractive walled town of Salvatierra is worth a visit and a base for exploring the area. The southern part of the province drops away to sunny plains, part of the Rioja wine region. Laguardia, the area's main centre, is not to be missed.

➻ *For listings, see pages 96-98.*

Western Alava → *For listings, see pages 96-98.*

West of Vitoria the green pastures give way to a rugged and dry terrain, home of vultures, eagles and dramatic rock formations. The area is served by bus from Vitoria.

Salinas de Añana

This hard-bitten half-a-horse village has one of the more unusual sights in the Basque lands. The place owes its existence to the incredibly saline water that wells up from the ground here, which was diverted down a valley and siphoned into any number of *eras* or pans, flat evaporation platforms mounted on wooded stilts. It's something very different and an eerie sight, looking a little like the ruins of an ancient Greek city in miniature. As many as 5500 pans were still being used by the 1960s but nowadays only about 150 are going concerns. The first written reference to the collection of salt in these parts was in AD 822, but it seems pretty likely the Romans had a go too.

During Semana Santa, Salinas comes to life; Judas is put on trial by the villagers. However, it's something of a kangaroo court as he's always convicted and burned.

Cañón de Delika

To the west beyond Salinas, and actually reached via the province of Burgos, is this spectacular canyon that widens into the valley of Orduña. The Río Nervión has its source near here and when running, it spectacularly spills 300 m into the gorge below: the highest waterfall in Spain. There's a good 90-minute round walk from the car park. Follow the right-hand road first, which brings you to the falls, then follow the cliffs along to the left, where vultures soar above the valley below. When you reach the second mirador, looking down the valley to Orduña, there's another road that descends through beech forest back to the car park. Near the car park is a spring, the **Fuente de Santiago**. Legend has it that St James stopped here to refresh himself and his horse during his alleged time in Spain. To get to the car park, which is about 3 km from the main road, the 2625 (running from Orduña in the north to Espejo in the south and beyond) turn-off is signposted 'Monte Santiago' and is about 8 km south of Orduña. There are buses to Orduña from Vitoria bus station with **La Unión**.

Eastern Alava → *For listings, see pages 96-98.*

The eastern half of the Alava plain is dotted with interesting villages, churches and prehistoric remains. The town of Salvatierra is the most convenient base for exploration or walking. At the northern fringes of the plain, the mountains rise into Guipúzcoa. One of the Camino de Santiago routes passes through the natural tunnel of San Adrián here.

Salvatierra/Agurain

The major centre in eastern Alava is the not-very-major Salvatierra (Agurain), a well-preserved, walled medieval town with some interesting buildings. Around Salvatierra there's plenty of walking, canyoning and abseiling to be done, while further afield canoeing, windsurfing, paragliding and horse trekking can be arranged. The sleeping and eating possibilities are nothing to write home about, but there are a couple of *pensiones*, both attached to restaurants. The **tourist office**, on the main street half a block up from the square with the **Iglesia de San Juan**, is very helpful. They currently hold keys for the churches in Salvatierra as well as the marvellous church at Gaceo. Unfortunately, though, they don't have permission to lend the keys to visitors so currently the only option is to pay for a guided tour. A guided trip to Gaceo and Alaiza costs €2 per person: contact Tura① *T945 312 535; www.agurain.biz*, for details. Tours run every Thursday and Sunday, and daily in July and August, but also by arrangement (50 per group).

Túnel de San Adrián and around

One of the most interesting walks starts from the hamlet of Zalduondo, 8 km north of Salvatierra. A section of the **Camino de Santiago**, part of it follows the old Roman/ medieval highway that effectively linked most of the peninsula with the rest of Europe. It's about 5.5 km from Zalduondo to a small parking area named **Zumarraundi**. From there, the track ascends through beech forest to the Túnel de San Adrián. Shortly after meeting the old stone road, there's a right turn up a slope that's easy to miss; look for the wooden signpost at the top of the rise to your right. The tunnel is a spectacular natural cave cutting a path through the hill. It houses a small chapel, perhaps built to assuage the fears of medieval pilgrims, many of whom thought that the cave was the entrance to Hell. After the tunnel, the trail continues into Guipúzcoa, reaching the attractive town of Zegama about 90 minutes' walk further on. There are numerous adventure tourism options in the area.

Eguilaz

The area around Zalduondo and Salvatierra is also notable for its prehistoric remains; in particular a series of dolmens. Near the village of Eguilaz 45 minutes' walk from Salvatierra (just off the N1 to the east) is the dolmen of **Aitzkomendi**, which was rediscovered by a ploughing farmer in 1830. What happened to the plough is unrecorded, but the 11 impressive stones making up the structure all tip the scales at around the 10-ton mark. It's thought that the dolmen is a funerary marker dating from the early Bronze Age. On weekdays, five buses run to Zalduondo from Vitoria/Salvatierra (destination Araia); two run on Saturday and one on Sunday.

Sorginetxe and around

On the other side of Salvatierra near Arrizala is the equally impressive Sorginetxe, dated to a similar period. The name means 'house of the witch'; in the Middle Ages when the area was still heavily wooded, it could well have been the forest home of somebody of that profession. To the east of here, near the village of Ilarduia, is the **Leze Cave**, a massive crevice in the cliff face. It's 80 m high and a stream flows from its mouth, making access tricky for casual visitors. It's a good place for canyoning (see **Tura**, in Salvatierra, above).

Gorbeia

North of Vitoria, straddling Vizcaya and Alava, is the massif of Gorbeia, an enticing and inaccessible area of peaks and gorges topped by the peak of the same name, which hits 1482 m. It features in Basque consciousness as a realm of deities and purity. There are several good marked trails around **Murguia**, including an ascent of the peak itself, which shouldn't be attempted in poor weather.

La Rioja Alavesa → *For listings, see pages 96-98.*

Basque Rioja? The two words don't seem to go together naturally but in fact many of the finest Riojas are from Alava province. Confusion reigns because the Spanish province of La Rioja is only one of three that the wine region of the same name encompasses. Although it's not far from Vitoria, the Rioja Alavesa definitely feels Spanish rather than Basque; the descent from the green hills into the arid plains crosses a cultural and geographical border. As well as the opportunity to visit some excellent wineries, the hilltop town of Laguardia is one of the most atmospheric places in Northern Spain.

Laguardia/Biasteri

The small, walled hilltop town of Laguardia commands the plain like a sentinel – which it was; it was originally called La Guardia de Navarra (the guard of Navarra). Underneath the medieval streets, like catacombs, are over 300 small bodegas, cellars used for the making and storing of wine, as well as a place to hide in troubled times. Most are no longer used – **Bodega El Fabulista** is a fascinating exception.

Even if wine is put aside for a moment, the town itself is captivating. Founded in 1164, its narrow streets are a lovely place to wander. Traffic is almost prohibited due to the bodegas carved out 6 m below. The impressive **Iglesia de Santa María de los Reyes** ① *weekend tours at 1730 and 1830, €2, at other times ask at tourist office*, begun in the 12th century, has an extraordinarily well-preserved painted Gothic façade, while the former Ayuntamiento on the arched Plaza Nueva was inaugurated in the 16th century under Carlos V.

Laguardia's **tourist office** ① *C Mayor 52, T945 600 845, www.laguardia-alava.com, Mon-Fri 1000-1400, 1600-1900, Sat 1000-1400, 1700-1900, Sun 1045-1400*, is in the centre of things.

Laguardia was the birthplace of the fable writer Félix de Samaniego.

Around Laguardia

The area around Laguardia also has a few non-vinous attractions. A set of small lakes close by is one of Spain's better spots for birdwatching, particularly from September to March when migrating birds are around. There are a series of marked walking and cycling routes in this area, spectacularly backed by the mountains of the Sierra Cantábrica.

If you're coming from Vitoria by car, it's marginally quicker and much more scenic to take the smaller A2124 rather than the motorway. After ascending to a pass, the high ground dramatically drops away to the Riojan plain; there's a superb lookout on the road, justly known as 'El Balcón' (the balcony). From here, the whole of the Rioja region is visible before and below you.

Wineries

Though not strictly a winery, **Centro Temático Villa Lucía**① *Ctra Logroño s/n, T945 600 032, www.villa-lucia.com, Tue-Sun 1000-1400, 1700-2000, €5-15*, is definitely a winey experience. It offers intriguing 'virtual' tasting sessions that'll help hone your skills, and you can also pre-arrange a variety of different tasting sessions of the real stuff. There's also a botanic garden here.

Bodegas Palacio

① *Ctra de Elciego s/n, T945 621 195, www.habarcelo.es, tours Tue-Fri 1200 and 1300, Sat 1100, 1200, 1300, €5 (redeemable in shop or restaurant); booking essential.*

One of the handiest of the wineries, and worth seeing, is **Bodegas Palacio**, located just below Laguardia on the Elciego road, some 10 minutes' walk from town. The winery is modern; the older bodega alongside having been charmingly converted into a hotel and restaurant. Palacio produces a range of wines, the quality of which has increased in recent years. Their *Glorioso* and *Cosme Palacio* labels are widely sold in the UK.

The winery was originally founded in 1894 and is fairly typical of the area, producing 90% red wine from the Tempranillo grape, and a small 10% of white from Viura (as well as *crianzas, reservas* and *gran reservas*, see box, page <?>). Palacio also produce a red wine for drinking young, *Milflores*, which is soft, fruity and a change from the woodier Rioja styles.

Bodega El Fabulista

① *Plaza San Juan s/n, Laguardia, T945 621 192. Tours daily at 1130, 1300, 1730, and 1900; Sun: mornings only, €6.*

A massive contrast to Palacio, which produces two million bottles a year, is **Bodega El Fabulista**, next to the tourist office in Laguardia. Eusebio, the owner, effectively runs the place alone and produces about 1/50th of that amount. The wine is made using very traditional methods in the intriguing underground cellar from grapes he grows himself. The wines, marketed as *Decidido*, are a good young-drinking red and white. He runs four tours a day, which are excellent and include lots of background information on the Rioja wine region and a generous tasting in a beautiful underground vault.

Herederos del Marqués de Riscal

① *C Torrea 1, Elciego, T945 180 888, www.marquesderiscal.com, multilingual tours Tue-Sat 1000, 1230, 1600, Sun 1100 and 1300, €10, reserve in advance.*

Founded in 1860, Marqués de Riscal is the oldest and best known of the Rioja bodegas and has built a formidable reputation for the quality of its wines. The Marqués himself was a Madrid journalist who, having cooled off in France after getting in some hot political water at home, returned to Spain and started making wine. Enlisting the help of Monsieur Pinot, a French expert, he experimented by planting Cabernet Sauvignon, which is still used in the wines today.

The innovative spirit continues, and Marqués de Riscal enlisted none other than Frank Gehry of Guggenheim museum fame to design their new visitor complex, a visual treat of a building which opened in 2006. Gehry's design incorporates ribbons of coloured titanium over a building of natural stone. The silver, gold and 'dusty rose' sheets are Gehry's response to 'the unbroken landscape of vineyards and rich tones'. The building encompasses a hotel, a restaurant, and an oenotherapy spa, which combines water treatments with applications of grape and vine extracts.

The winery is modern but remains faithful to the bodega's rigorous tradition of quality. As well as their traditionally elegant *Reserva* and *Gran Reserva*, the more recently inaugurated *Barón de Chirel* is a very classy red indeed, coming from low-yielding old vines and exhibiting a more French character than is typical of the region.

Buses from Vitoria to Logroño via Elciego pass through here and Laguardia, which is 7 km away.

Other wineries

Two kilometres north of Laguardia, with a waved design echoing the steep mountains behind it, is **Ysios Bodega** ① *T945 600 640, www.domecqbodegas.com/ysios, visits are daily at 1100 and 1300, €5, they need to be pre-arranged*, designed by Santiago Calatrava, the brilliant Valencian engineer/architect who seems to have made Euskal Herría his second home.

Twenty minutes east of Laguardia is the pretty but parched town of Oyón/Oion. One of the bigger operations here is **Bodegas Faustino Martínez** ① *T945 622 500, www. bodegas faustino.com, tours weekdays during working hours and Sat 1100, 1300, phone to arrange, €6*, whose range of Faustino wines are a reliable and popular choice both in Spain and the UK. They run a good tour of their operation in Spanish or English. The tour is all the better for being a bit more in-depth and a little less cursory than some of the other big wineries.

Alava Province listings

For Sleeping and Eating price codes and other relevant information, see pages 12-19.

🛌 Sleeping

Salvatierra *p93*

€€ Eikolara, Barrio Arbinatea 30, Zalduondo, T945 304 332, www.eikolara.com. An excellent *casa rural*, this great spot is a characterfully restored old stone house in the village of Zalduondo. The rooms (which vary in price and size) are colourfully and stylishly decorated, and the owners are helpful and keep it all super clean and ship shape. Breakfast included.

€€ Zadorra Etxea, C Zadorra 21, T945 312 427, www.zadorraetxea.com. Although often let out whole over weekends, this *casa rural* does offer accommodation on a per-room basis. Friendly owners and thoughtful decoration with exposed beams and wooden floors make this Salvatierra's best place to stay.

€ Mendiaxpe, Barrio Salsamendi 22, Asparrena, T945 304 212, mendiaxpe@terra. es. Cleverly located in the wooded foothills

of the Sierra de Urkilla, this is a superb base for walking in the area. There's use of a kitchen but no meals available except breakfast. The 3 en suite rooms are lovely and light.

€ Merino, Plaza de San Juan 3, T945 300 052. One of 2 unremarkable *pensiones* in Salvatierra, it offers a *menú del día* in its restaurant.

La Rioja Alavesa *p94*

There are some excellent places to stay in Laguardia.

€€€€ Hotel Marqués de Riscal, T945 180 880, C Torrea 1, Elciego, www. starwoodhotels.com. This flamboyant structure is visible from afar and is your chance to stay in a Frank Gehry-designed building. The exuberant waves of metal conceal a modern building made from traditional stone. The rooms are, as you'd expect at this price, well designed if not enormous, and have appealingly offbeat shapes and features. You'll get better rates from the website the further in advance you book. There's also a fine gourmet restaurant.

€€€ Hospedería de los Parajes, C
Mayor 46, Laguardia, T945 621 130, www.
hospederiadelosparajes.com. Right in
the heart of the old town, this recently
opened hotel offers significant style and
comfort and peaceful rooms with excellent
facilities. There's a range of room classes
at different prices and sizes, but all boast
chic fabrics and modern-rustic design
and great bathrooms. There's a wonderful
underground bodega that makes a
romantic spot for an evening glass of
local wine.

€€€ Castillo El Collado, Paseo El Collado 1,
Laguardia, T945 621 200, www.hotelcollado.
com. Decorated in plush but colourful style,
this mansion at the north end of the old
town is comfortable and welcoming. There
are 10 individually decorated rooms as well
as a restaurant. The owner is more than
helpful, and can arrange your bodega visits
for you. Recommended.

€€€ Posada Mayor de Migueloa, C
Mayor 20, Laguardia, T945 621 175, www.
mayordemigueloa.com. A beautifully
decorated Spanish country house, with
lovely old wooden furniture and a peaceful
atmosphere. Rooms are heated and a/c. The
restaurant is of a similarly high standard.

**€€ Hotel Antigua Bodega de Don Cosme
Palacio**, Carretera Elciego s/n, Laguardia,
T945 621 195, www.hotelcosmepalacio.
com. A wine lover's delight. The old **Palacio
Bodega** has been converted into a charming
hotel and restaurant, adjacent to the
modern winery. The sunny rooms are named
after grape varieties, and come with a free
½ bottle. Most rooms feature views over the
vines and mountains beyond and have a/c
to cope with the fierce summer heat. The
rates are reasonable too.

€€ Hostal Biazteri, C Berberana 2,
Laguardia, T941 600 026, www.biazteri.com.
Run by the owners of the bar on the corner,
this is a very airy and pleasant place to
stay. Rooms are spacious, comfortable and
reasonably priced. Breakfast is included.

€ Larretxori, Portal de Páganos s/n,
Laguardia, T945 600 763, larretxori@
euskaltel.net. This comfortable *agroturismo*
is just outside the city walls and commands
excellent views over the area. The rooms are
spruce, clean and good value and the owner
is very benevolent.

🍴 Eating

La Rioja Alavesa *p94*

♦♦♦ Mesón La Cueva, Concepción 15, Oyón
(La Rioja), T945 601 022. If you're visiting
wineries over this way, a hearty lunch here is
in order. It's a place with a lofty and deserved
reputation in the heart of the village, with a
new upstairs *comedor* which is light and airy,
a significant improvement. The *menú* is €22
but features some excellent Riojan staples,
such as *pochas* (young broad beans) and
other hearty stews. Recommended.

♦♦ Castillo El Collado, Paseo El Collado 1,
Laguardia, T945 621 200. There's an excellent,
well-priced restaurant with 3 attractive eating
areas in this beautiful fortified hotel at the
northern end of Laguardia.

♦♦ El Bodegón, Travesía Santa Engracia 3,
Laguardia, T945 600 793. Tucked away in
the middle of old Laguardia is this cosy
restaurant, with a €11 *menú del día* focusing
on the hearty staples of the region, such as
pochas (beans) or *patatas con chorizo*.

♦♦ Marixa, C Sancho Abarca s/n, Laguardia,
T945 600 165. In the **Hotel Marixa**, the
dining room boasts great views over the
vine-covered plains below and has a range
of local specialities with formally correct
Spanish service.

🍸 Bars and clubs

La Rioja Alavesa *p94*

Café Tertulia, C Mayor 70, Laguardia. With
couches, padded booths and a pool table,
this is the best place for a few quiet drinks
in Laguardia.

O Shopping

Laguardia *p94*
La Vinoteca, Plaza Mayor 2, T945 621 213. A worthwhile wine shop in the centre of town.

⊖ Transport

Salinas de Añana *p92*
Bus 5 buses daily from **Vitoria** bus station.

Salvatierra *p93*
Bus There are **Burundesa** buses hourly from **Vitoria** bus station to Salvatierra, 40 mins.

Gorbeia *p94*
Bus There are 4-5 daily buses to Murguia from **Vitoria** bus station.

La Rioja Alavesa *p94*
Bus There are 3-4 daily buses to Laguardia from **Vitoria** bus station (1 hr 45 mins). These run via **Haro** and proceed to **Elciego** and **Logroño**. There's 1 daily bus from **Bilbao** that stops here (1 hr 45 mins, €11.05), but no return service; you'd have to go to **Vitoria** or **Logroño**.